Baking
Soda

Hundreds of Everyday

This is a **FLAME TREE** book
First published in 2011

Publisher and Creative Director: Nick Wells
Project Editor: Catherine Taylor
Picture Research: Katie Pimlott, Catherine Taylor, Harrison Fertig
Art Director: Mike Spender
Layout Design: Jane Ashley
Operations Manager: Chris Herbert

Thanks to Laura Bulbeck, Theresa Bebbington, Polly Prior, Daniela Nava, Helen Snaith

13 15 17 16 14

3 5 7 9 10 8 6 4

This edition first published in 2013 by
FLAME TREE PUBLISHING
Crabtree Hall, Crabtree Lane
Fulham, London SW6 6TY
United Kingdom

www.flametreepublishing.com

© 2012 Flame Tree Publishing Ltd

ISBN 978-0-85775-094-5

Printed in Singapore

Baking Soda

Hundreds of Everyday Uses

Diane Sutherland, Jon Sutherland, Liz Keevill and Kevin Eyres

**FLAME TREE
PUBLISHING**

Contents

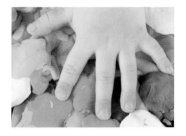

Introduction

If you could find a naturally occurring product that you could use as a deodorant, a toothpaste, an exfoliant, and an antiseptic, you'd be impressed. If you found out that you could use the same substance in the kitchen to make a big improvement to many of your favorite dishes, and then use it to clean out your pots and pans, leaving them grease free and shining, you'd be amazed. And if you were told that exactly the same product could be used to shampoo your pets, clean out your swimming pool, kill cockroaches, and relieve insect bites and stings, you'd probably just laugh. Well, there is just such a product, it's been around for thousands of years in one form or another, and you can by it today for pennies.

It All Started in Ancient Egypt

When the ancient Egyptians needed something that would keep mummified bodies dry and free from bacteria on their journey through the afterlife, they found the answer: a sodium compound occurring naturally in dry lake beds. They called the substance Natron because a particularly good source was an area called Wadi-el-Natrun.

The Egyptians quickly discovered that Natron could also be used as an extremely effective cleaner around the home. Not only that, but blended with olive oil it made soap; in its natural state it could be used as toothpaste and diluted it made a breath-freshening antiseptic mouthwash.

What's more, they found that Natron burned with a smokeless flame when mixed with castor oil—handy for working in tombs without leaving soot stains. And it was useful in chemical processes, such as glass-making. All in all, a pretty remarkable and versatile substance.

Then Came Pearlash and Soda Ash

Over the centuries the various elements that make up Natron were refined down to more specific substances for individual uses. Late in the eighteenth century, European chemists discovered that another form of sodium, pearlash, was particularly useful in dramatically speeding up the baking process. However, the production of pearlash involved the burning of huge amounts of wood to produce ash, and pretty soon wood for pearlash was in short supply.

In 1791, French chemist Nicolas LeBlanc produced a process for turning common salt (sodium chloride) into soda ash (sodium carbonate), a substance with the same characteristics as pearlash but without the need to burn vast tracts of woodland.

And Finally There Was Baking Soda

American bakers loved soda ash and North America was soon producing its own. However, American soda ash couldn't match the quality of the European product so American bakers were forced to import large quantities of European soda ash.

All that changed in the 1830s, when an American, Austin Church, began experimenting with new ways of producing high-quality sodium bicarbonate. Church, a doctor, developed a process that converted purified sodium carbonate into food-grade sodium bicarbonate

Giving up his medical practice, Church joined forces with his brother-in-law, John Dwight, moved to New York, and founded John Dwight & Co. Dwight called his sodium bicarbonate "saleratus" (aerated salt) and was soon selling it to bakers and housewives across the country.

Thirty years later Austin Church retired from the business a rich man, but he wasn't finished with sodium bicarbonate.

With his two sons he set up Arm & Hammer to produce baking soda products, and if you go into any pharmacy or supermarket, you can still find Arm & Hammer toothpaste on the shelves.

You Can Call It:

- baking soda
- bread soda
- bicarbonate of soda (more commonly used in the United Kingdom)
- bicarb (again, more commonly used in the United Kingdom)
- sodium bicarbonate
- saleratus
- or even, sodium hydrogen carbonate

But Don't Confuse It With:

- caustic soda (sodium hydroxide)
- baking powder (although it does contain baking soda)
- sodium chloride (common salt)
- sodium carbonate (also known as washing soda, or soda ash)

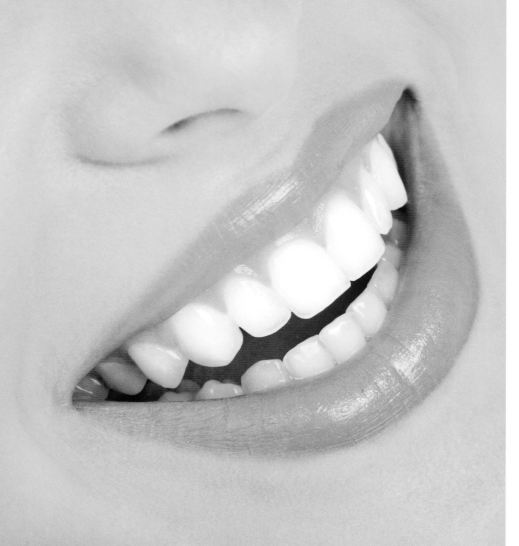

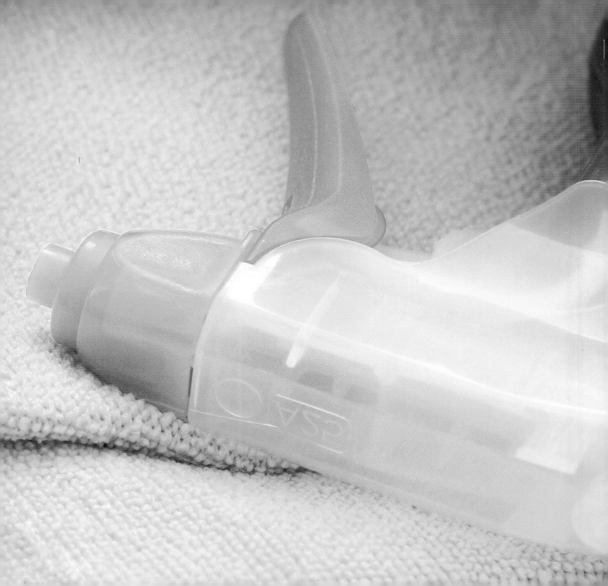

Cleaning

Kitchens

If you glance at the ingredients of most of the cleaning products that live under your sink, you will find a scary list of some truly horrendous-sounding chemicals, many refined from gasoline and most of them highly toxic. It doesn't have to be like that. Baking soda used in various ways, straight or diluted, can replace many of those cleaners at a fraction of the price and at considerably less risk to your health. Here's how…

Cleaning dishes

End that Sinking Feeling

For effective, eco-friendly dish washing, simply add 1 tablespoon baking soda to a sinkful of hot water and swish in the juice of half a lemon. If you use commercial dish-washing liquid, add a couple of tablespoons (or more) of baking soda to the water to boost its action. This is really effective when dealing with greasy dishes.

A Handy Stand-By

Keep a little bowl of dry baking soda close to the sink. If you encounter a stubborn stain, dip your dishcloth, brush, or sponge in and scrub—the offending mark will be gone in no time. This doesn't just work on china and pans but is also great for glass and plastic cookware.

 CAUTION: Do not use on nonstick finishes.

And Here's Another One

Add some baking soda to a flour or sugar shaker and keep it by the sink. Use it to sprinkle on stains, then scrub and rinse. Or recycle a plastic scouring powder or talcum powder container and use to hold dry baking soda. Whatever kind of container you use, be sure to label it carefully so it doesn't get mistaken for food.

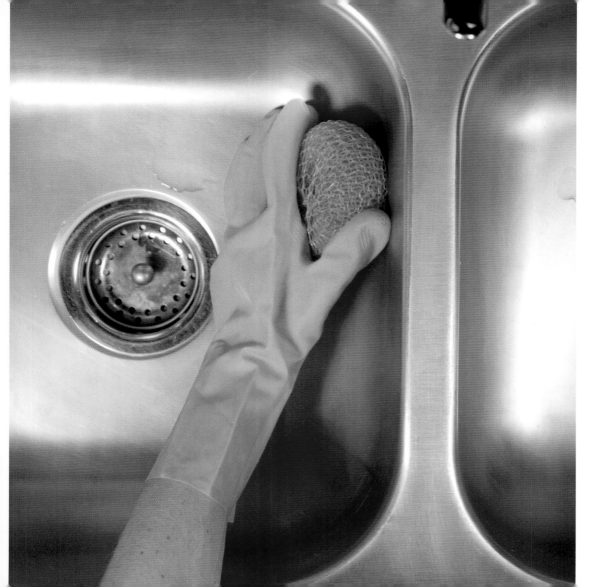

Banish Dirty Dishcloths and Washed-up Sponges

Rinse dishcloths and sponges after use in a solution of hot water and baking soda to keep them smelling like roses. Occasionally soak overnight for an extra powerful freshening up. Always dry cloths thoroughly before putting away to keep them hygienic and to avoid the buildup of unpleasant smells.

Up to Your Elbows in Hot Water?

Keep those rubber gloves smelling like daisies by sprinkling a little baking soda into them each time you take them off. Not only will it absorb any dampness and keep them fresh for next time, they will also glide on and off like a dream.

In the Dishwasher

Why spend money on multicolored tablets with a ball stuck in the middle for no apparent reason? Make up your own dishwasher powder by putting 2 tablespoons baking soda and 2 tablespoons borax into the powder compartment for a full load.

What Is that Smell?

To freshen up a smelly dishwasher and give it a thorough clean, sprinkle about 150 g/5 oz/ ¾ cup baking soda into the bottom of the machine and run it empty through a complete hot cycle. Smell gone.

And reduce odor buildup between cycles by sprinkling about a handful of baking soda over the dirty dishes and onto the bottom of your dishwasher.

Clean Plates but Dirty Dishwasher?

For stubborn stains in your dishwasher, use dry baking soda on a damp cloth or sponge, or mix up a paste with baking soda and a little water and use like cream cleaner. This is particularly effective for getting rid of that nasty gunk that builds up around the hinges, rubber door gaskets, and in other hard-to-reach areas of dishwashers. Rinse well to remove any residue.

Welcome Home

No one wants to return to a smelly dishwasher after they've been on vacation, so sprinkle a little baking powder into the empty machine and leave the door slightly open. It will be a delight to come back to.

Give Cutting Board Smells the Chop

Cutting boards can acquire a less-than-pleasant smell over time, so give yours a regular spring cleaning by shaking over about

3 tablespoons of baking soda and sprinkling with just enough water to moisten. Let stand for about 15 minutes to absorb those onion and garlic odors, then rub well with a wet sponge. Rinse in clean water and let dry.

Pots and Pans

For those boring things that won't go in the dishwasher, mix together equal quantities of baking soda, borax, and salt, and use as a scouring powder that will cut through the heaviest grease and grime on pans, broiler pans, and baking sheets

Remember to rinse well afterward, and don't use on nonstick surfaces, such as Teflon, because it will damage them. Baking soda will also tend to make aluminum pans turn darker.

Don't Want to Wash Them Right Now?

Alternatively, soak dirty pots and pans in a basin of hot water with 2 or 3 tablespoons baking soda for about an hour. Then scrub them clean with an abrasive scrubber. Again, not for nonstick, under any circumstances.

Left a Pan on the Heat and Forgotten About It?

To remove seriously burned-on food, soak the pan in baking soda and water for 10 minutes before washing. Or scrub the pot with dry baking soda and a moist scouring pad. Don't use abrasive cleaners on nonstick housewares.

For a really scorched pan with burned-on food in the bottom, scrape off as much of the debris as you can, then pour a thick layer of baking soda directly into the pan. Moisten the baking soda with a little water, then let soak overnight. This should loosen the burned food and you'll just need to scrub clean and rinse. If this still doesn't work, boil a strong solution of baking soda in the pan for about 10 minutes. This should soften up the burned food sufficiently for you to scrub it away with some dry baking soda on a damp scourer.

What About Nonstick?

For burned pans that you don't want to scrub, such as nonstick, bring a mixture of water and 250 ml/8 fl oz/1 cup vinegar to a boil in the pan. Remove from the heat and add a couple of tablespoons of baking soda. Let soak overnight, then wipe clean and rinse well.

Mugs and Cups

Use a paste of baking soda and water to remove tea and coffee stains from ceramic and melamine cups. Let the solution soak in the cup for a while, then rub and rinse. So much more ecological than bleach, and it doesn't leave an aftertaste.

Surfaces

Work on those Counters

Wipe your kitchen counters over with a little dry baking soda sprinkled onto a damp cloth or sponge. Rinse with clean water and wipe dry. It's a safe and natural way to keep surfaces clean and leaves them free of taint.

Alternatively, mix up a solution of baking soda and hot water and use this to wash down your counters, leaving them sparkling and fresh. Rinse and dry as above. Rinse your cleaning cloths or sponges in the same solution and dry thoroughly before putting away.

Freshen up Formica

To erase stains on laminate counters, such as Formica, use a thick paste of baking soda and rub gently until the offending mark disappears. Rinse well to remove the white residue. If that doesn't fix it, squeeze some lemon juice onto the stain, let stand for around half an hour, then add a little dry baking soda to the lemon. Rub with a sponge, rinse clean, and dry.

Shining Sinks

Sinks come up sparkling and bright when you clean them with baking soda. Use dry on a damp cloth, or make up a paste with baking soda and water, and use like cream cleaner.

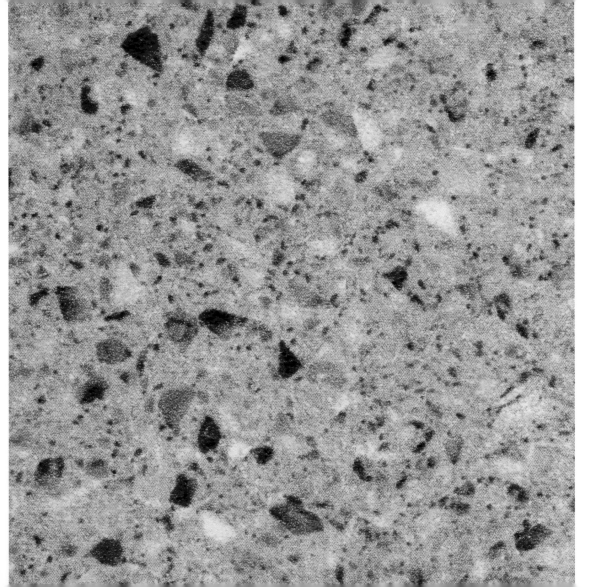

Degrease Lightning

Prevent the buildup of grease in your kitchen sink drain by regularly putting a large handful of dry baking soda down it. Do this about once a month for best results, and make sure you do it just before you set off on vacation so there are no nasty drain smells on your return.

Alternatively ...

Keep your sink drain fresh by regularly putting a handful of baking soda down the drain with the same amount of salt, and follow it down with a cupful of boiling water. Let soak for about half an hour, then pour down a whole saucepan of boiling water.

Back to White

If your porcelain or white enamel sink has taken on an unpleasant yellowish tinge, get it looking like new by mixing 1 L/1¾ pts/1 qt warm water with 50 g/2 oz/¼ cup soda and 120 ml/4 fl oz/½ cup chlorine bleach. Pour into the sink and let soak for a quarter of an hour. Keep children and pets away while you are doing this. Then rinse well until the bleachy smell goes completely.

 CAUTION: Keep children and pets away while you are doing this. Rinse well until the bleachy smell goes completely.

Dispense with Dirty Waste Disposals

Keep waste disposal units clean by switching the unit on and running hot water through it. While it is still running, add a handful of baking soda, then keep the faucet running until all traces of powder have disappeared.

Appliances

Top Stove-top Tip

Make a paste of baking soda and water and use like a cream cleaner on a sponge or cloth. Wipe over well to remove all white streaks and rinse with clean water. Alternatively, dampen the stove-top or burner thoroughly and sprinkle with baking soda. Let stand for half an hour to absorb any grease, then rub clean with a sponge or cloth and rinse well. Wipe over glass stove-tops with a solution of hot water and baking soda on a sponge or cloth. Tackle any stubborn marks or burned-on food with dry baking soda on a wet cloth.

Detox Your Oven Cleaner and Your Oven

Proprietary oven cleaners can be highly toxic, and often contain caustic chemicals that give off dangerous fumes. Not nice. However dirty your oven is inside, baking soda can beat the burned-on grime. Scrape off as much gunk as you can, then mix plenty of baking soda with a little water to make a thick paste. Spread this over the sides and bottom of the cold oven and let soak overnight. Wipe down the next day with hot water and repeat if necessary. Use dry baking soda on a scourer or sponge to deal with really stubborn areas, rinsing well afterward.

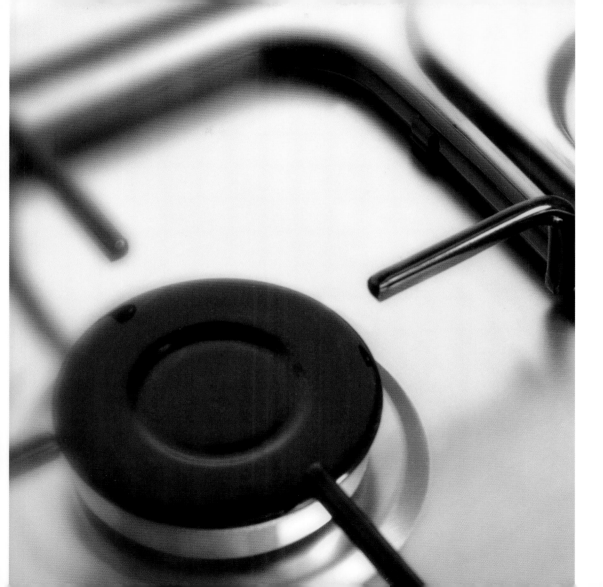

Oven Spritzer

Another way to keep ovens fresh and clean is to spray the interior of the oven with water (a plant or laundry sprayer works well for this), then sprinkle with dry baking soda. Spray again to dampen the powder. Give additional spritzes with water every hour or so, let the mixture soak overnight, and then remove with a cloth. Rinse with hot water.

Can't See through that See-through Door?

Glass oven doors can get so splattered with grease and grime that you can't see through them any more. Get them crystal clear again by scrubbing with baking soda on a damp cloth or sponge. Rinse well and dry.

Microwave Maxi Cleaning

Insides of microwaves can get sprayed with overenthusiastically heated food, leaving them smelling musty, especially when the door is kept closed. To refresh your microwave without leaving any taint or chemical smells, remove the turntable plate, if there is one, and wash this in the sink in a solution of hot water and baking soda, then dry.

Wipe over the inside of the microwave with a solution of 1 L/1¾ pts/1 qt hot water and 4 tablespoons baking soda. Be sure to wring your cloth or sponge out before wiping, because you don't want water to get into the workings through any little perforations in the inside of the oven.

Tackle stubborn splashes with dry baking soda on a damp cloth or sponge and rinse clean. Dry the inside of the microwave and replace the turntable. You can wipe down the outside using the same solution.

More Microwave Magic

Another way to freshen your microwave is to add a couple of tablespoons of baking soda to a half-full cup or mug of hot water (make sure the cup or mug is microwave-safe). Put in the oven on full power and boil for around 5 minutes. The steam will condense on the inside of the warm oven, loosening splatters of food and leaving it damp. All you need to do is wipe over with paper towels, a cloth, or sponge, and then dry.

If you must leave your microwave door closed when it's not in use, you can eliminate musty smells by leaving a small open container of baking soda inside. A ramekin, cup, or glass, or yogurt container is ideal. Just remember to remove it before using the oven and replace it afterward. Stir the contents each time you do and replace the whole lot every 2–3 months.

Freshen up Your Refrigerator

Refrigerators need a complete spring clean every now and again, especially if something has turned rotten in there and the smell just won't go away. Remove all the food, shelves, drawers, and containers, and wipe them over, along with all surfaces and nooks, with a solution of hot water and baking soda on a clean cloth or sponge (an old toothbrush is

useful for difficult crannies, and you can use dry baking soda on a wet brush for stubborn marks). Rinse and dry carefully before switching the appliance back on.

If you need to leave a refrigerator switched off, leave the door propped open and put an open container of baking soda inside.

And Don't Forget the Freezer

If you have to defrost your freezer, wipe it over inside with a solution of 4 tablespoons baking soda to 1 L/13/4 pts/1 qt warm water. Wipe over all surfaces and dry before turning the freezer back on.

If your freezer is frost-free, it can be tempting to leave it for eons without cleaning it. However, even frost-free freezers appreciate a wipe down inside from time to time. Use the same solution as above.

Clean on the Inside, Clean on the Outside

Kitchen appliances, ovens, refrigerators, dishwashers, and so on can get amazingly grimy when you're not looking. Wipe the whole lot over regularly using a solution of baking soda and warm water. Use a cloth or sponge and wring out to avoid drips.

Odor Removal

Refrigerator (Odor) Magnet

Strong cheese is great, but things like that can leave a not-so-great smell in the refrigerator. Fight back by leaving an open container of baking soda in there to absorb strong smells and eliminate stale odors. Stir the contents regularly and replace every 2–3 months, or you'll find the baking soda itself is starting to smell!

A Fresher Salad Drawer

While you're dealing with the refrigerator, sprinkle the bottom of the salad drawer with a little dry baking soda, then cover with a layer of paper towels. Wipe out and change every three months.

Clean Your Thermos

Get rid of musty or unappetizing smells in a thermos by simply adding a teaspoonful of baking soda, filling it with hot water, then letting it soak for at least 30 minutes. Empty and rinse well with cold water. And leave the top off if you're not going to use it for a while.

And a Fresher Air Freshener

Fill a small bowl almost to the top (choose a pretty one for added effect) with baking soda and add a few drops of your favourite essential oil. Place anywhere in the house that you need to keep things smelling sweet. Add more oil when the effect starts to wane and replace the whole lot about every three months.

When it isn't convenient to have an open bowl around (such as under a sink), cut the feet off a clean old pair of tights and fill the foot with baking soda. Knot the leg and place this inside the other cut-off foot. Knot again and put it anywhere you need to eliminate stale smells.

Smelly Hands?

If you've just been chopping onions or garlic, peeling potatoes, or handling fish, it can be difficult to erase the smell, even with soap. Baking soda will get rid of the odor—sprinkle some onto wet hands, rub together well, and rinse off.

Onion Odor Eaters

Remove the odor of onion and garlic from wooden or other porous surfaces by sprinkling

some baking soda onto a damp cloth and rubbing it into the surface. Rinse with water, or let stand for about half an hour to work for stronger smells.

Plastic Food Containers

Plastic can absorb strong smells and less-than-appetizing odors can build up in plastic food containers, especially if they are left closed or weren't scrupulously clean when put away. Banish those musty odors by washing the container in a hot-water-and-baking-soda solution, then sprinkle about three tablespoons of baking soda into the bottom of the container and fill with hot water. Put the lid on and shake gently over the sink, then let stand for at least a couple of hours to work. Rinse out and wash again as usual.

Seasonal Smells

Musty smells can build up in food containers that are only used during certain times of the year. To prevent this, sprinkle the insides of picnic hampers and cool boxes with a little baking soda before putting away. Wipe out with a damp cloth before using.

Ban Smelly Trash Cans

If your kitchen trash can has a nasty smell that just won't go away, make a solution of 200 g/7 oz/1 cup baking soda in warm water. Pour it into the trash can and fill with more warm water. Let it soak for an hour or two, then empty down a drain or the toilet. Make sure you rinse and dry carefully, because bacteria and mold (the cause of bad smells) multiply much faster in warm, steamy conditions.

To prevent smells from building up in the first place, sprinkle a little baking soda in the bottom of the trash can, then line the bottom with a couple of sheets of newspaper, before inserting a (biodegradable) trash can liner.

If a liner leaks, don't ignore it. Deal with it right away by wiping out the trash can with a baking-soda solution and rinsing with clean water. Change the newspaper and baking soda regularly, every month or so, to keep things really fresh.

And Bread Box Mold

Accumulated crumbs in the bottom of a bread box can easily turn moldy (ugh). Make sure you empty them out regularly and wipe over the inside of the box with a solution of baking soda and warm water. Remember to dry the box out thoroughly and let it cool before you place fresh bread in it, or the mold will return.

Bathrooms

The bathroom is a place to pamper yourself as well as keep clean, so it's really important that you keep it spotless and germ-free. And because they're often damp and steamy, bathrooms easily attract mildew and mold, and no one wants to stare at those when they're soaking in the bathtub. Because your skin comes into contact with the surfaces, the bathroom is the last place you want to use toxic chemicals for cleaning, so it's time to reach for that container of baking soda again.

General

Complete Clean

For general bathroom cleaning, including the bathtub, basin, shower tray, and wall tiles, mix a paste of baking soda and water and use it like a cream cleaner on a damp cloth or sponge.

And get rid of more stubborn stains with dry baking soda on a damp cloth or sponge. Rinse well to remove any streaks and wipe dry.

Sweet Smells

Baking soda is perfectly safe for all surfaces, and a couple of drops of essential oil added to the cleaning mix will add extra freshness, so no need for harmful air sprays. Give lemon, pine, tea tree, or ylang-ylang a try.

Grimy Nonslip Strips?

Nonslip strips are a useful safety measure but difficult to keep looking spotless. You'll find they get dingy after a while, which may also make them less effective. The answer? Wet the strips and sprinkle with baking soda. Let work for about half an hour, then rub clean with a sponge or cloth and rinse well. Job done.

Say Good-Bye to Bathroom Odors

Musty smells can lurk in bathroom cabinets and cupboards, particularly under basins where there might be slight leakage from pipes and faucets. Keep your bathroom storage areas smelling fresh by putting a small, open container of baking soda in each one; this will also help absorb damp.

If you use baking soda as an air freshener in your bathroom, remember to replace it about every three months, but don't throw it in the trash—pour it down the toilet, let soak for a while, then flush to help clean the toilet.

Leaving an open bowl of baking soda outside the bathroom or by the toilet will help to absorb any nasty smells. Choose a pretty container that goes with the room decor and, again, replace the contents about every three months. Add a few drops of essential oil for a luxurious touch.

Banish Musty Bathroom Trash Cans

Bathroom trash cans can quickly get a little musty, which is both unhygienic and unpleasant. If your trash can is washable, rinse it clean with a solution of baking soda and dry carefully. All trash cans, whether washable or not, will definitely benefit from a sprinkle of baking soda in the bottom, covered with a piece of paper towel. Tip or wipe out the powder about every three months and replace the paper as necessary.

Bathroom Hardware

Tap Dancing

If you live in a hard-water area, there's a good chance that there's a lime-scale deposit around the taps on the faucet—annoying and hard to remove. Not anymore—mix some baking soda with a little vinegar and brush the fizzy paste on the offending areas. Let stand for about half an hour then rub gently and rinse clean. This works equally well for all hard-water marks in the bathroom, including on glass shower screens.

Keep Your Drains Running Clear

Regular drain cleaning helps minimize unpleasant smells and guards against blockages. Keep your drains clear by mixing two parts baking soda, two parts salt, and one part distilled white vinegar and pouring the solution down the drain in your bathtub, basin, and shower. Put in the plugs and let the mixture froth away merrily for about half an hour, then run the hot faucet to rinse. Easy.

Bath Time

Baking soda is safe for cleaning all types of bathtubs, but you probably don't always want to bother cleaning it straight after you've had a soak. No problem: Just sprinkle a couple of tablespoons of baking soda into the bathwater before you pull out the plug and your bath will be as clean as you are.

Shower Power

Any shower cubicle can be cleaned quickly and effectively with a baking-soda-and-water paste. If you're feeling lavish, add some shampoo or shower gel to the mix for a nice smell.

If you live in a hard-water area, you'll know that glass shower doors soon get covered in annoying water marks. Don't worry: Just wipe the glass over with a little distilled white vinegar on a cloth or sponge, and then rub over with a sprinkle of baking soda. Rinse well and then squeegee the glass for streak-free spotlessness you can be proud of. Keep a squeegee in the shower and get all the family to have a quick run over the surfaces with it after each shower. It'll cut down on cleaning a lot.

Clear Your Head

Another common problem in hard-water areas is blocked showerheads—not what you need first thing in the morning. If you're able to remove the head, soak it in a mixture made up of 250 ml/8 fl oz/1 cup vinegar with 3 tablespoons baking soda in a suitable container slightly bigger than the head until the lime scale has completely dissolved.

If for any reason you can't remove the head to clean it, pour the baking-soda-and-vinegar mixture into a strong plastic bag, a little bigger than the showerhead, and tie or tape it in place over the head so it's in close contact with the frothy solution. Leave in place for the mixture to work its magic for about half an hour, then remove the bag and rinse the head with clean warm water. Run water through the head to clear any residue and you'll soon be singing in the shower again.

Curtains for Moldy Shower Curtains

A moldy shower curtain is the last thing you want flapping around when you're trying to get clean. Soak yours regularly in warm water with about 5 tablespoons baking soda (the bathtub is a good place for this). Give it a slosh around a few times, then squeeze out and hang to drip dry. Always let shower curtains dry flat after washing, otherwise you'll find the mold will be back again. Not nice.

For moldy patches or stubborn stains, make up a thick paste of baking soda and rub clean using a sponge, cloth, or old nailbrush or toothbrush.

Machine-washable shower curtains can be washed on the gentle setting with 100 g/3½ oz/ ½ cup baking soda or half that amount of mild washing powder and the same of baking soda. Throw in some towels to absorb the suds and water, and wash the curtain (which is probably waterproof!) more effectively. Adding 250 ml/8 fl oz/1 cup distilled white vinegar to the rinse cycle will help.

 CAUTION: Don't use the spin cycle or you could end up with a permanently creased curtain (and shower curtains aren't usually designed to be ironed). Drip

dry in an airy place (outside is ideal) or hang it back up in the shower and leave the window open.

Be Kind to Your Toilet

Commercial toilet cleaners use harsh, caustic chemicals, such as bleach, which can stain your clothes if it splashes, harm your hands, and, of course, end up in the water supply. Be gentle with your toilet by sprinkling some baking soda around the bowl, let stand for about half an hour, and then scrub with a toilet brush and flush.

Remove more stubborn marks by sprinkling the toilet bowl with baking soda and pouring a dash of distilled white vinegar on top. Use a toilet brush to scrub the bowl clean with the bubbling froth that results.

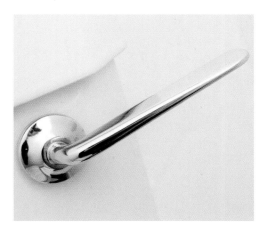

Sitting Comfortably?

Any kind of toilet seat will look as good as new when wiped over with a mild solution of baking soda. Don't forget to do the underneath of the seat and lid, too. When you've finished, pour the rest of the solution down the toilet for a really thorough clean.

Flushed with Success

Every few weeks sprinkle some baking soda in your cistern. Let soak overnight, then flush the next day for a sparkly clean toilet.

Furniture & Surfaces

Our homes are under constant attack from dust, germs, and bugs, let alone pets, children, and the occasional party. Couches, chairs, curtains, and cushions all have to put up with a lot of mistreatment, walls are often on the receiving end of grubby hands (tiny or otherwise!), and floors can suffer from spills and simply from people walking around in shoes designed for sidewalks or the park, not the parquet. Bring all these surfaces back to life with a few handfuls of baking soda.

Furniture

Back to White

White and light painted furniture can quickly lose its original brightness. Make it look as good as new by wiping it with a solution of 2 tablespoons baking soda to 1 L/1¾ pts/1¼ qts warm water. Scrub black marks off chair legs with a paste of baking soda and water. Rinse and dry.

Ring Remover

Get rid of cup rings and other heat marks on wooden furniture by gently rubbing with a baking soda and water paste. If this doesn't work, add a pea-size blob of toothpaste for extra abrasion. Make sure you don't get the furniture wet because this may cause further stains. Wipe over, dry carefully, and, finally, buff with some furniture polish.

Dry-Clean Your Three-Piece Suite in Fifteen Minutes

To give any fabric upholstery a quick dry-clean, sprinkle the surfaces generously with baking soda (use a flour shaker or empty talc container). Leave for about 10 or 15 minutes to absorb any stale odors, then vacuum up all the powder.

Mix baking soda and soap in a bowl. Dilute with water and add vinegar. Stir with a fork until lumps dissolve. Pour into a spray bottle and shake well.

Scouring Powder

1 cup baking soda
1 cup borax
1 cup salt

Combine ingredients in a plastic container with a tight lid. Mix well.

Toilet Bowl Cleaner

1 cup borax
½ cup white vinegar

Flush toilet. Sprinkle borax around bowl, then liberally drizzle vinegar on top. Let sit undisturbed for 3 to 4 hours, then scrub with toilet brush. Flush to rinse.

Tip: For tougher jobs, make a paste from ⅔ cup borax and ⅓ cup lemon juice. Apply to toilet bowl. Let sit for 2 hours, then scrub.

Drain Opener

½ cup baking soda
1 cup vinegar
1 teaspoon boiling water

Pack drain with baking soda, then pour in vinegar. Keep drain covered for ten minutes. Flush with boiling water.

you threw away more than $2,000 worth of food last year. That's about one fourth of the food and drinks we buy, reports the Natural Resources Defense Council (NRDC). A smart way to cut down on waste is to plan your meals for the week, starting with dishes that use up anything you already have and need to eat quickly. Then buy only any remaining ingredients. Dana Gunders, a scientist at the NRDC, has compiled more tips in the book *Waste-Free Kitchen Handbook: A Guide to Eating Well and Saving Money by Wasting Less Food*. Learn more and buy the book at danagunders.com. ℝ

With additional reporting by Lauren Cahn

37 Try Walmart's produce again.

If you've avoided fresh fruits and vegetables at Walmart, you might want to reconsider. Greg Foran, Walmart's U.S. president and CEO, says the company has worked hard to cut down the number of days it takes produce to land in stores—by two to three days for most, four days for strawberries.

38 When is that cooked chicken a bargain?

Despite some reports that buying a rotisserie chicken is cheaper than roasting your own, that's not always true. A comparison by priceonomics.com

One way to save money on household items is to make them yourself. It's easier than you think. Our new book *Homemade* has recipes for cleaning products that work as well as the brands, which can be expensive (and filled with chemicals).

■ Window Cleaner

⅓ cup white vinegar

¼ cup rubbing alcohol

3¾ cups water

Mix ingredients in a spray bottle. Shake well.

■ Furniture Polish

1 cup olive oil

⅓ cup lemon juice

Combine ingredients in a spray bottle. Shake well.

■ Multipurpose Cleaner

3 cups water

⅓ cup rubbing alcohol

1 teaspoon clear household ammonia

1 teaspoon mild dishwashing liquid

½ teaspoon lemon juice

■ Dishwasher Detergent

2 cups borax

2 cups washing soda

Combine ingredients (find both in the laundry aisle) in a plastic container with a tight lid. For each load of dishes, put 2 tablespoons of the mixture into the dishwasher soap dispenser.

Tip: For sparkling dishes, pour white vinegar into the rinse compartment.

■ Bathroom Cleaner

1⅓ cups baking soda

½ cup liquid soap

½ cup water

2 tablespoons white vinegar

size isn't necessarily the biggest value. The key is to look for a unit price below the price on the shelf—the price per ounce or liter or whatever. In some cases, the medium-sized package might be your winner.

30 Hoard at the holidays.

Supermarkets often offer their deepest discounts around holidays and food-centric events such as the Super Bowl, so stock up then.

31 Claim your group discount.

If you're over a certain age, you may be eligible for a senior discount—typically 5 percent—if you shop on the right

27 Don't fall for fake sales.

Beware sneaky tactics that stores use to lure you into buying more. "We'll take an 89-cent can of tuna and mark it 'ten for $10,'" says Jeff Weidauer, a former supermarket executive. "Instead of buying six cans for 89 cents apiece, people will buy ten for $10."

Degrease

Annoying grease marks on cloth upholstery can be made to vanish by sprinkling with one part baking soda and one part salt. Simply brush the mixture in lightly with an old toothbrush, then let it work overnight to absorb the stain. Vacuum up the next day.

Alternatively ...

Make a paste of 1 tablespoon water and 3 tablespoons baking soda and rub into stains on fabric seat covers—an old toothbrush works well. Let the mixture dry, then brush carefully with a clean dry brush and vacuum away any residue.

 CAUTION: It is best to test the mixture first on an inconspicuous area to check that the fabric is colorfast and that it won't affect the surface of the fabric or leave watermarks.

A Cure for Under-the-Weather Leather and Vinyl

Leather and vinyl furniture often has a textured finish that can trap grease and dirt, leading to a generally grimy effect. Revive the finish by mixing 1 tablespoon baking soda with 250 ml/ 8 fl oz/1 cup warm water and use on a cloth or sponge to wipe down the furniture. Blast

more stubborn grime with a paste of baking soda and water. Rubbing this into all the nooks and crannies will leave everything sparkling clean. Wipe over well with clean water on a sponge or cloth and dry.

Metal Furniture

Grimy metal furniture can be brought back to life by cleaning with a paste of baking soda and water on a cloth or sponge. Rinse clean and dry carefully to prevent rust formation.

Rust-Buster

If rust does appear on metal furniture, wipe over the affected area with a paste made from 1 tablespoon baking soda and a few drops of water on a damp cloth. Then polish with a piece of aluminum foil, wipe down with a clean damp cloth, and dry carefully with paper towels.

Lackluster Laminates?

Any laminate surfaces that are looking a bit dull will respond well to being spruced up with a damp cloth or sponge sprinkled with baking soda. Rinse and dry.

Floors & Walls

All Floors

Looking for an excellent general-purpose, hard-floor cleaner that costs pennies? Try dissolving a handful of baking soda in a bucket of warm water and use as normal on a floor mop. Wring out well to avoid saturating the surfaces, then stand back and admire the finish.

Good for Wood

Water can damage parquet and other solid wood floorings. To remove any offending watermarks, take a damp cloth or sponge and sprinkle a little baking soda onto it, then rub carefully. Wipe over with a well wrung-out cloth or sponge and dry carefully.

 CAUTION: Don't get the floor wet—this will obviously cause further problems.

Lifeless Lino, Vinyl or Cork Flooring?

Unsightly scuff marks from dark shoe soles on lino, vinyl flooring, and cork tiles will vanish when rubbed with a paste of baking soda and water.

Crying Over Spilt Ink?

It's no use crying over spilt ink—you just have to do something about it. For spills on hard surfaces, wipe up as much ink as possible, then sprinkle with baking soda. Let soak for a few minutes to absorb any residue, then add more powder and rub at the stain with a wet cloth or sponge. For stubborn stains, moisten the powder with a little vinegar instead of water.

On the Carpet

The sooner you deal with any stain, the better your chance of successfully removing it. This applies just as much to carpets as anything else. If you spill wine or drop grease on your favorite Axminster, sprinkle the area with baking soda (or one part baking soda and one part salt), brush in gently and let it absorb the stain for several hours. Sweep up the powder with a clean brush, then dab with a solution of baking soda and warm water. Let dry completely, then vacuum the area.

Routine Measures

If you're going to vacuum the carpet, it will be much fresher afterward if you sprinkle it with baking soda first. Let it sit for about 10–15 minutes, or better still overnight, to work, then vacuum the carpet until all traces of powder have disappeared.

Preventive Strike

Before having a new carpet laid, vacuum the bare floor carefully, then sprinkle it all over with baking soda to help keep your carpet smelling fresh. Make sure you tell the fitters not to sweep up the powder, though.

That's Sick

Cleaning up vomit is never a pleasant job, but bring baking soda to the rescue and you can ensure there are no lingering nasty memories. Get your rubber gloves on (sprinkling a little baking soda inside them for freshness and ease of removal) and scrape up as much mess

as possible, then cover the area with a layer of baking soda. Let soak for a few minutes, then scrub from the edges toward the middle with a sponge or brush moistened repeatedly in clean warm water. Sprinkle the area again with baking soda and let dry, then vacuum up the powder.

The antibacterial action of baking soda will deal with any residual odors, even on carpet. This process also works well with urine.

If you can't clear up vomit immediately because you're in the middle of an emergency, throw some baking soda over the affected area to curb nasty smells; deal with it as soon as possible.

Removing "Artwork" from Walls

To clean marks, such as those from crayon, pencil, marker pens, or grease, off washable walls, make a solution of baking soda and warm water and wipe over. If any children's masterpieces or other stains prove hard to remove, sprinkle dry baking soda on a damp cloth or sponge and scour gently.

 CAUTION: It's a good idea to test out on an inconspicuous area of wall first, just in case the finish isn't as washable as you thought.

Washable Wallpaper

Rub stains on washable wallpaper with a paste of baking soda mixed with a little water. However, bear in mind there is washable and washable, so in case your paper is "wipeable" rather than "scrubbable", always test on a less noticeable part of the wall first.

Revive Dull Tiles

Wipe dull, lifeless tiles over with a solution of baking soda, and see them spring back to their old shiny selves. Use the powder dry on a wet cloth or sponge for more stubborn stains and to clear soap residue. When you've finished, rinse with clear water and wipe or squeegee dry.

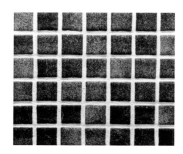

Defeat Grubby Grouting

Grubby grouting will never show your bathroom in its best light. Revive stained tile grout with a thick paste of baking soda and an old toothbrush. Make sure you rinse the whole area clean when you've finished to remove any white streaks.

Alternatively, for general discoloration on tile grout, make up a fizzy paste using two parts baking soda and one part distilled white vinegar or lemon juice. Apply the paste to the grout with an old toothbrush, let soak for 10 minutes, and then rinse the whole lot off with warm water.

If your grout has stubborn stains that simply refuse to budge, it's time to use a big gun. Moisten the baking soda with bleach instead of water (but not more than one part bleach to three parts baking soda) and scrub the grout with this, rinsing well afterward and wiping.

 CAUTION: If you do decide to use the bleach mixture as a last resort, you will need to take a few simple precautions: open the window and wear rubber gloves and old clothes, wash any splashes off your skin immediately, keep the mixture away from children and pets, and, of course, make sure you dispose of any leftover mixture safely.

Windows

First Class Glass

It's amazing how dirty windows can get without our noticing. Get in the habit of washing your windows regularly with a wet cloth or sponge sprinkled with a little baking soda. Rinse over with clean water and polish with a crumpled sheet of newspaper until dry, which will help remove any watermarks or smears.

And don't forget the frames. Wipe them down with a mixture of one part vinegar to two parts baking soda. This is especially effective if condensation has left areas of mildew.

Beautiful Blinds

Washable blinds (do make sure they are washable) will return to their just-bought glory once you've doused them in a bathtub of warm water and 250 ml/8 fl oz/1 cup

baking soda. Wipe away the dirt with a sponge or dish-washing brush (give the cords a quick scrub, too), then rinse down using the showerhead or take outside and give a gentle blast with the garden hose. Hang the blind up to dry.

 CAUTION: Place an old towel in the bottom of the bathtub first to prevent the blind from scratching or marking it.

Mirror, Mirror on the Wall

Like windows, mirrors can quickly loose their luster. Baking soda is great for returning grubby mirrors back to their gleam.

See yourself in a new light by sprinkling a little baking soda on a damp sponge or cloth and rubbing over the mirror. Wipe over with a clean cloth or sponge and fresh water, then polish with a crumpled newspaper for a sparkling, smear-free finish.

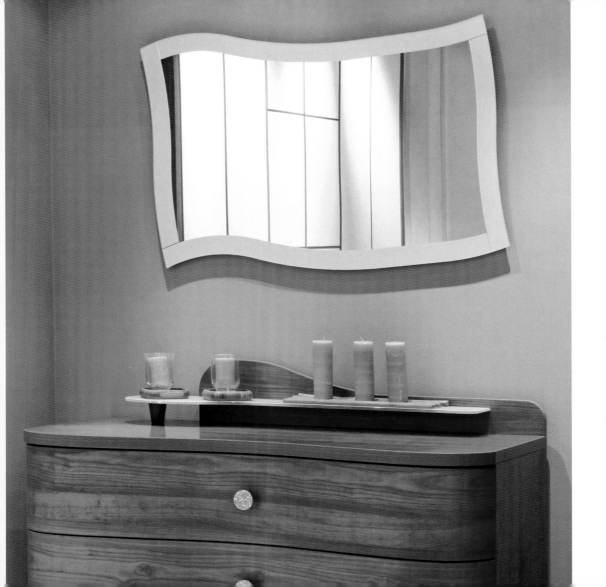

General Household

Wherever the water goes when we empty a sink or bathtub, or flush the toilet, you can send it swiftly on its way, making sure there aren't any lingering, unpleasant smells with a dash of baking soda. Not especially glamorous maybe, but vitally important for our health and well-being. And baking soda is great at neutralizing the smell of things around the house, such as shoes, sneakers, and pets that are making their presence felt a bit too much.

All-purpose Cleaner

Drain Training

If the water isn't draining away as fast as it normally does, or you suspect you've got a blockage, it's time for action. Pour about 100 g/3½ oz/½ cup baking soda down the sink swiftly followed by about 120 ml/4 fl oz/½ cup of distill white vinegar. Put the plug in while the chemicals froth up in a rather satisfying way. Let bubble away for a couple of hours, then pour down a saucepan of boiling water. Used regularly, this combination will break down the fatty acids that block drains and help to keep them smelling fresh as a daisy.

Going on Vacation?

Don't forget to put a handful of baking soda down all drains in the home before you go away for any longer than a couple of days. It'll prevent your neighbors from suffering any unpleasant bad drain smells while you're gone, especially in hot weather, and it will make your place much nicer for you to come home to.

Skeptical about Septic Tanks?

If you've got a septic tank, don't worry. Baking soda is best for keeping it in tip-top shape. In fact, it positively helps the process of breaking down waste by keeping the contents at the correct pH level, which favors the right kind of bacteria. Baking soda also helps protect the fabric of the tank from corrosion that can be caused by too-acid an environment. So, if you're not connected to a main sewage system, put a handful of baking soda down the toilet each week and give your tank a healthy treat.

Metal Cleaning

Silver Lining

Stop using unpleasant chemicals on your silverware. Instead, banish tarnish by applying a paste of water and baking soda, or dry baking soda on a damp cloth or sponge. Rinse or wipe with clean water and dry.

Adding a tiny squeeze of mild detergent or shampoo to the baking soda paste when you're cleaning the family silver will give you even more cleaning power. Rub, rinse, and polish dry.

If you're lucky enough to have some large, flat pieces of silverware, cut a potato in half and dip into baking soda. Rub over the surface of the silver, then polish clean with a soft cloth.

The Family Jewels

You can clean several small items of solid silver jewelry together by placing them in a suitably sized flat glass dish lined with a piece of slightly scrunched-up aluminum foil.

Arrange the jewelry on the foil, ensuring each piece is in contact with it. Sprinkle the pieces with baking soda. Then boil some water, let it cool slightly, and pour over the items until they are all submerged. Turn the items over gently so all surfaces are in contact with the foil in turn. The tarnish will transfer to the foil. Magic.

Get Stainless Steel and Chrome Really Stainless

Bring any stainless steel and chrome surfaces back to life with a sprinkle of baking soda on a damp cloth or sponge. If you've got "brushed" stainless steel surfaces, these have a grain so be sure to rub in the right direction. Wipe away any residues with a clean damp cloth and buff up to a good-as-new shine with a dry cloth.

Brassed off with Your Copperware?

Bring copper, brass, or bronze back to new by mixing three parts baking soda and one part lemon juice or white vinegar and cleaning with a soft cloth. But remember that if you're polishing brass, you must make sure it is uncoated or it won't work.

Copper Bottoms?

Clean copper pans by cutting a plump fresh lemon in half and dipping it in baking soda. Rub the surface of the pan in a circular motion. Wipe clean with fresh water and dry carefully.

The Ring of Confidence

Rings can get clogged up and grimy from daily contact with oily deposits from skin, hand cream, soap, or other cosmetics. Bring your precious jewels back to pristine condition by soaking them in a solution made from 1 tablespoon baking soda thoroughly mixed with a cup of tepid water.

 CAUTION: Don't use this method on pearls, or on jewelry where the gems may be glued in place rather than set in claws. If in doubt about submerging jewelry, rub gently with a baking soda paste using an old, soft toothbrush. Rinse and dry carefully before putting away.

Odor Removal

Smelly Carpets?

Carpets and rugs can get very musty, especially if you have pets. The solution is to sprinkle with baking soda the night before you vacuum. Sleep sound in the knowledge that the baking soda is hard at work absorbing smells. Vacuum as normal the next day.

Get It off Your Chest

Some people like that evocative Lion-the-Witch-and-the-Wardrobe smell that comes from old wooden furniture, but no one likes the way the smell can transfer to clothes, making them feel less than fresh. Banish the smell to Narnia by sprinkling some baking soda in the bottom of the piece of furniture, let it soak overnight, and vacuum out in the morning, then sprinkle in a bit more and place clean paper over the top.

Banish that dreadful smell of decaying mothballs that hangs about in some ancient furniture by filling a pomander with baking soda, or equal quantities of baking soda and borax, and hanging it up in the closet or wardrobe.

Alternatively ...

If you're feeling creative, or short of cash, make a sachet from old clean tights with baking soda, or fill a small container and stand it in the corner of the cupboard. Well-washed plastic food containers, or small sturdy cardboard boxes with holes punched in the lid, filled with baking soda are ideal. Having a lid makes it less likely to be tipped over and spilled.

Blanket Measures

If blankets smell musty when you take them out of storage, sprinkle them with baking soda and fold them up. Leave them overnight, then shake out in the yard and hang in the sunshine, or give them a 20-minute twirl in the clothes dryer on a low setting.

A Bed of Roses

Mattresses can get musty, especially if not used for a while—not a pleasant place to lay your head. Get rid of the fug by removing the mattress cover if there is one, dusting the mattress with baking soda, and leaving it overnight before vacuuming it up. Turn the mattress over and repeat the process.

Add a further sprinkling of baking soda before you put back the mattress cover (it goes without saying you've washed it!) and make up the bed. Pillows will benefit from the same treatment.

Butt Out

If you're a smoker, sprinkling a layer of dry baking soda in your ashtrays offers a double whammy. Not only does it absorb unpleasant smoky odors, but it also works as a fire extinguisher, so helps put smoldering butts out. Unfortunately, it won't do anything about cleaning up your lungs.

Musty Footwear

Let's face it, sneakers, shoes, boots, and slippers can start to smell if not taken care of properly. Avoid embarrassing stinky feet by sprinkling a couple of tablespoons of baking soda into each shoe and shaking carefully to distribute throughout its whole length. Empty into the toilet before wearing (the powder, that is, not the shoes) to keep your toilet smelling fresh as well.

For a potentially less messy solution, make sachets to go in your shoes to keep them fresh. The simplest way is to pour some baking soda into the foot section of old tights, knot at the ankle, and trim. Put one in each shoe when you're not wearing them.

Sprinkling a bit of baking soda on your feet (and in your socks) before you put your shoes on will help deal with footwear odor at the source if you are prone to this problem.

Game, Set and ... Smell

Sport and swimming bags can smell truly
ghastly if they're not kept aired and free of
dirty or wet gear. Avoid the shame of
stinky gear-bagitis by sprinkling the inside
of the emptied bag with baking soda. Let it
work overnight, then vacuum out. Sprinkle
a bit more in the bottom and leave it there
to absorb moisture and bad odors.

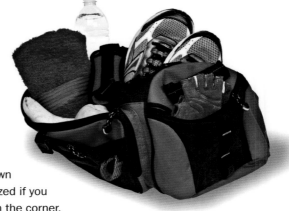

And if you're a member of a gym with your own
locker, it will stay fresh and much more civilized if you
put a small open container of baking soda in the corner.

Upstairs, Downstairs

Attics and basements often have a characteristically damp, musty smell. Tights to the
rescue again: Cut the legs off and fill the foot section with baking soda. Add another layer of
tights to make a double thickness, and then knot firmly. Use the rest of the leg to make a
loop and attach it to a rafter, beam, or hook. It might look odd (actually, it does look odd) but
it does the trick.

Love Your Luggage

Suitcases, trunks, travel bags, and other items of luggage often get stored for months at a
time and can get a musty smell, especially when left in the attic. When you get your luggage

down for a trip, sprinkle a little baking soda inside the day before you pack, let it work overnight, and vacuum thoroughly in the morning.

If spots of mildew appear on superior-looking leather luggage that's been left in storage or damp conditions, bring it back to its rightful position in life by gently rubbing the affected areas with a paste of baking soda and water. Dry off with a clean cloth, let dry thoroughly, then buff up with a suitable colored polish.

Tame that Tome

Old books can be yet another source of unpleasant musty odors. Use an old librarian's trick once you're sure the book is dry, and sprinkle lightly throughout with baking soda. Let it work on the book for a few days, then shake out the powder. The result: a book it's a pleasure to get your nose stuck into again.

Accidental water spills can cause the pages of books to buckle and stick together, but don't despair. Dry out wetness (or dampness) on paper by sprinkling the affected pages with baking soda and let the book dry on a sunny windowsill or another warm place, turning the pages regularly.

Pets

We all love our pets; that's a given. But sometimes they can smell less than fragrant, and occasionally they disgrace themselves when we're not looking. Wet dogs, cat litter, and hamster cages all have their unique aroma, and it's not one that adds to the pleasure of relaxing at home. Reach for the baking soda, and they'll soon be your best friends again.

Bathing & Floors

Washing, Wet or Dry

Give your pooch a quick dry-clean by sprinkling him (or her, of course) with a little baking soda and brushing it through the coat. Probably best done in the yard, this will absorb grease and remove those doggy smells you don't want to smell.

For a wet wash, add a couple of tablespoons of baking soda to the water when you bath your dog. This solution can be used by itself, when it will also help heal any skin conditions, or with a dash of shampoo. You won't need to use as much shampoo as usual, because the baking soda makes it work much more effectively. Rinse thoroughly after shampooing.

A Cleaner Vacuum Cleaner

Every time you change the bag on your vacuum cleaner add 1 tablespoon baking soda. And if it's the bagless type, just drop the baking soda into the dirt collection chamber. This will quickly curb that less-than-fresh smell that can linger when the cleaner starts to get full, especially if you have a dog in the house.

Whoops

When man's best friend leaves a nasty smell on the carpet, sprinkle on some baking soda. Let it work for half an hour then vacuum up. The baking soda will also help stop those doggy smells gathering in your vacuum cleaner.

Worse Than Whoops

After a night on the tiles, or swallowing too much fur, your cat can sometimes be sick and will seldom, if ever, use the litter tray. Wherever your cat decides to throw up, a solution of baking soda and water will not only clean up the mess, it should also remove any stains and unpleasant smells.

The Worst

If one of your pets leave something unspeakable on the carpet, scrape up or dry up as much as you can, then scrub the whole area with a solution of baking soda and warm water. Sprinkle the area liberally with more baking soda and let it work overnight, vacuuming up any residue the next day.

Getting rid of that telltale smell quickly will discourage the little darlings from soiling the same spot repeatedly.

Pets' Accessories

Kitty Litter

With the best will in the world, most us don't manage to clean out litter trays quite as often as we should. Luckily, baking soda will absorb those telltale cat litter odors if you plan ahead.

Next time you change your cat's tray, cover the bottom with a layer of baking soda and then sprinkle the cat litter on top. Be generous with the baking soda; the best arrangement is a ratio of around one part baking soda to four parts of litter. Add a little extra baking soda each time you remove anything between changes.

And So to Bed

Pet's beds and bedding can get dirty and start to smell. Freshen up your pet's sleeping arrangements by sprinkling with baking soda, leaving for at least 10 minutes, then vacuuming. Be sure to remove Fido first

Blanket the Smell

Pet blankets can be home to some particularly powerful odors that even a good hot wash won't always remove. Bring your blankets back to smell-free cleanliness by adding 100 g/3½ oz/ ½ cup baking soda to the detergent, either for machine or hand washing.

White-Collar Pets

Dogs' collars and leashs can get grimy and greasy over time, so scrub with a solution of baking soda and warm water. Nylon collars and leashs can be soaked in the solution if you prefer. This also works well on those plastic toys that your pet loves gnawing on.

How Clean Is Your Cage?

Next time you clean out a small pet's cage, sprinkle a layer of baking soda on the bottom before covering with a layer of newspaper, then bedding. Tank-style cages can be washed out with a solution of baking soda and warm water and rinsed in the bathtub or shower.

Feathered Friends

Birds can get salmonella and other similar gastric problems if you don't keep their feed hoppers and drinking containers spotless.

Wash these carefully in a hot-water-and-baking-soda solution and rinse and dry carefully before replacing. Use the same solution, rather than strong-smelling detergent, to clean out the cage.

Thanks for All the Fish (Tank)

Fish don't like it if their water becomes too acidic, so test the water with a special kit regularly and add a pinch or so of baking soda to correct the level if necessary.

And when you need to clean the tank, baking soda and water in paste form is perfect for scrubbing it out. It's safe and leaves no taint.

 CAUTION: Make sure you rinse the tank out carefully before refilling.

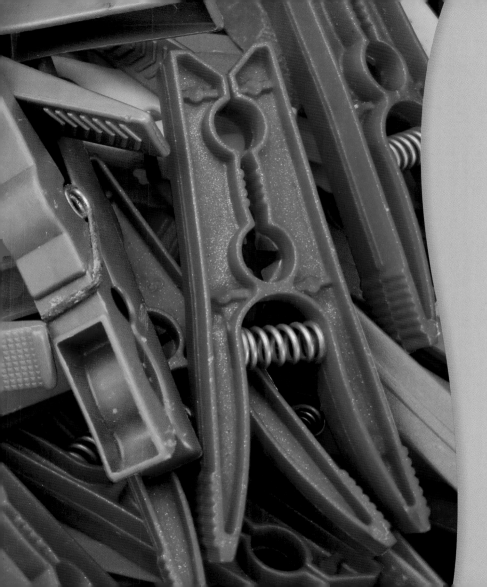

Laundry

Washing

Sparkling clean, sweet-smelling laundry is one of life's great pleasures. But as detergent manufacturers compete to bring us cleaner, brighter, whiter, fresher laundry at lower temperatures, they simply add more and more chemicals to their powders. In the long run, this leads to fabrics not lasting as long and an increasing number of people finding they're allergic to washing powders. Baking soda is a simple, inexpensive solution—its mildly alkaline formation means it dissolves dirt and grease, leaving laundry soft and clean.

Cleaning Clothes

Painless Stain Removal

Any type of stain is always best dealt with before it has time to dry because once the mark starts to set it will become much more difficult to remove. Because of its unique formulation, baking soda is great for many types of stain removal as well as for general laundry.

 CAUTION: Some fabrics that are optimistically described as machine or hand washable are really not suitable for this kind of washing at all. To be on the safe side, always test stain removal techniques on an inconspicuous area of the material first, especially if it is your absolute favorite item of clothing.

Blood Simple

Bloodstains are always difficult to remove, as anyone who watches TV crime shows will tell you. Baking soda, however, will normally remove blood from washable clothing. For small areas

of blood, dampen the stain with cold water—not hot water because this sets bloodstains, making them far more difficult to remove. Rub baking soda into the stained area with an old toothbrush or clean nailbrush. Let the baking soda paste soak for a while and repeat the process if necessary. Launder as normal

Blood Not So Simple

For larger areas of blood, add 200 g/7 oz/1 cup baking soda and 250 ml/8 fl oz/1 cup distilled white vinegar to a bucket of cold water. Swirl the mixture around well, then add the bloodstained clothing. Let soak for several hours—overnight is ideal—then launder as usual.

Vomit and Urine

There's no nice way to say this, but vomit and urine are acidic. The first thing to do is thoroughly rinse any stains under cold running water as soon as possible after the event to avoid lasting damage to the fabric. Sprinkle the area with baking soda and let stand for

about half an hour before washing. Baking soda will neutralize the acid and prevent it from permanently damaging clothing.

For larger areas of vomit, scrape off as much as you can, then soak the item or items in a bucket of cool water to which you have added 200 g/7 oz/1 cup baking soda.

Couldn't Face Cleaning It at the Time?

If acidic stains or spills have dried onto clothes, don't soak them in water because the acid will be reactivated and will start to harm the clothes. This explains why clothes that have had acid splashed on them go into the wash intact and come out with holes.

Instead, mix some baking soda with a little water and spread onto the stain. This will neutralize the acid before it has time to start eating into the fabric. Let the baking soda soak for an hour or two, then wash as normal.

This also works for other acid spills, such as lemon, orange, and other citrus juices (which, although they're good for you, are acidic), acidic toilet cleaners, and battery acid. You can also try this for wine spills and other fruit stains.

No Sweat!

Scrub those unpleasant perspiration stains from washable clothing with a nailbrush and a paste of baking soda and water, let soak for at least an hour to work effectively—longer for bad stains—then wash as normal. Not only will this remove the stain, it'll get rid of the smell, too.

Rusty Clothing?

Rust isn't just a problem for suits of armor. Rust stains can also appear on suits made of cloth and other clothing. Soak the area with lemon juice, then sprinkle generously with baking soda. Let soak overnight to work, then rinse off and wash as normal.

Ease off Grease

Grease stains can be so frustrating. They just seem to come back wash after wash. Don't despair: sprinkle fresh grease splashes with baking soda and let soak for an hour or two to work. Then drip a little water onto the powder and scrub gently. Rinse off and wash as normal.

For dry-clean only clothes, just sprinkle the dry powder on as above, let it soak to work, and brush off with a clean, soft brush.

Ballpoint Blobs?

Ballpoint pen or other types of ink can be removed from leather clothing but you need to act fast. Sprinkle a little baking soda on the stain, let soak for a couple of hours to absorb the ink, then brush off and buff up the leather.

Gray-Collar Worker?

Greasy, discolored shirt collars and grimy cuffs will soon be dazzling white if you scrub them with a paste of baking soda and water and a nailbrush. Let the mixture soak for half an hour or so, then wash as normal.

For severe stains, try drizzling a little distilled white vinegar onto the soaking mixture. The resulting froth will deliver the extra grease-busting power that you need.

Persuade Suede to Come Clean

Suede is all too easy to stain and expensive to dry-clean. Before you head to the cleaners, try gently rubbing dry baking soda into stains on the suede, using a soft brush. Let it set, then brush off carefully. It makes sense to try this on an inconspicuous part of the garment before you proceed to ensure it doesn't have any adverse effects.

New Baby, New Clothes

New baby clothes often contain a dressing that stiffens the fabric so it looks good in the store. Perversely, this can cause soreness and rashes on delicate baby skin. Rinse this unnecessary chemical concoction out of the clothing before the bambino wears it by washing the garment in warm water and a little mild detergent to which you have added 100 g/3½ oz/½ cup baking soda.

Some adults also find their skin is irritated by these fabric dressings, so just follow the same instructions.

Happy Diapers

Disposable diapers can leave a dubious ecological legacy. If you are using the traditional cloth alternative, soak the dirty diapers in baking soda and water overnight. This not only curbs unpleasant smells, but means that you can use less detergent in the machine when it comes to washing them.

In the Swim

Remove damaging chlorine or salt from your swimsuit after a trip to the pool or swimming in the sea by soaking the garment for an hour or two in warm water to which you have added a handful of baking soda. Wash as usual and your swimwear will keep looking good for much longer, and it won't have that worryingly bleachy smell when you next put it on

Tune up Your Washing Machine

Adding 100 g/3½ oz/½ cup of baking soda to a load of laundry will improve the performance of your usual liquid detergent, helping with the removal of stains and grease. And, because baking soda acts as a very effective water softener, you'll find you will get the same results with considerably less detergent than usual.

What's more, your white clothes will come out looking whiter, and brightly colored clothes will keep their color longer. All for a few pennies.

Reduce Rashes

If, in common with many people, you're allergic to commercial laundry powders and find they irritate your skin, try using 200 g/7 oz/1 cup baking soda in your laundry instead. This is also ideal for getting baby clothes nice and soft.

A Handy Hand-Washing Tip

You can hand wash delicate articles in warm water with 50 g/2 oz/¼ cup baking soda and about a tablespoon of hand-washing laundry liquid. Wash and rinse as usual, adding a tablespoon of baking soda to the final rinse as a softener.

 CAUTION: Before you wash anything delicate, you should pay particular attention to the washing instructions that came with the garment.

A Soul Mate for Your Soleplate

The soleplate of your iron can easily get marked and hard water will soon block up the steam holes. Remedy this by unplugging the iron and leaving it to cool, then rub over the plate with baking soda and water paste on a sponge or cloth. Wipe over with a clean damp cloth and buff dry.

Odor Removal

Smoke Gets in Your Clothes

To remove smoke smells from clothes, whether from cigarettes or barbecues, add 100 g/ 3½ oz/½ cup baking soda to the rinse cycle. This will also get rid of the smell of mothballs or musty closets that might be lingering on your clothes.

Alternatively, soak smoky clothes in a solution of baking soda before you put them in the washing machine. This works well for clothes tainted with smoke, or clothes that haven't been dried properly and have developed a horribly rancid "old dishcloth" smell

Perspiration Inspiration

Baking soda not only deals with sweat stains but also banishes the smell, too. This can be a real boon because work clothes and sports garb can still retain that acrid smell (sorry, there's no nicer way to describe it) even after normal laundering. Soak offending items overnight in a solution of 100 g/3½ oz/½ cup baking soda and 4 L/7 pts/1 gal warm water before laundering as usual.

Damp Patches

If there are areas of mildew on clothing that's been in storage, rub with a paste of baking soda and water before washing.

Pampered Hamper

Banish the whiff of musty laundry hampers by sprinkling baking soda over the dirty laundry. This also prevents the hamper itself from becoming smelly. Add another handful of baking soda each time you put another load of grubby clothing in.

Feeling Creative?

Putting a homemade sachet into your laundry hamper will absorb unpleasant smells for months. Simply cut out a circle of lightweight fabric, about the size of a dinner plate, and place a large handful of baking soda in the center. Add some lavender or a few drops of your favorite essential oil. Gather the fabric up around the powder and secure with a rubber band. Tie a ribbon around the band to hang against the side of the hamper or drop it into the bottom. Nice.

Sick Note

Sorry to mention it again, but the smell of vomit has a nasty habit of lingering on clothing, even after laundering. Scrape off as much as possible, run the affected area of the garment under running water, then sprinkle the area liberally with baking soda and let soak for about an hour. Scrub and rinse, then launder as normal.

Dunk the Skunk

If you ever have the unpleasant experience of being squirted by a skunk, you'll be tempted to put all your clothes in the trash can—and preferably one several miles from your home. Stop: You may be able to rescue them if you act quickly. Try soaking the stinky clothes overnight in a solution of 100 g/3½ oz/½ cup baking soda to 4 L/7 pts/1 gal water, repeat if necessary, then wash as normal.

Give Your Washing Machine a Vacation

If you find your washing machine smells less than fresh when you get back from your vacation, sprinkle a little baking soda and leave the door open overnight. Next morning, clean the inside and outside of your washing machine and tumble dryer with baking soda sprinkled on a damp cloth or sponge.

Next time you go away, sprinkle in the baking soda before you go. No need to rinse out—just let it stay in there for the next wash.

Condition & Color

Getting clothes clean is important, but so is the condition and color of your laundry when it comes out of the machine (or the sink, if you're hand washing). Try these simple ways to get your laundry looking as good as new, and you'll soon have softer, brighter, more vibrant clothes.

Soft & Bright

Soften It Up

Baking soda not only washes clothes, but works well as a fabric softener. Its gentle action is ideal if you find commercial fabric conditioners irritate your skin, or you want to avoid all that plastic packaging. Try adding 100 g/3½ oz/½ cup baking soda at the rinse stage or mix with a little warm water and pour into the conditioner drawer of your washing machine. It leaves clothes smelling fresh, but without the artificial, perfumed smell of store-bought softeners. Baking soda as a softener is really good for keeping towels fluffy and soft.

Alternatively, mix two parts water, one part baking soda, and one part distilled white vinegar. It will fizz up like mad, but once it has calmed down completely you can pour in into a plastic bottle for storage. Be sure to label it clearly and keep it out of the reach of children. Add about 50 ml/2 fl oz/¼ cup of the mixture to the fabric softener drawer in your machine per wash

Whiter Than White

If you habitually add bleach to the detergent in your washing machine, also add 50 g/2 oz/ ¼ cup baking soda if you are using a front-loading machine, or twice as much for top loaders. Your usual bleach will not only work harder, but you will only need to use half the quantity that you normally do. Your white wash will come up brighter, and baking soda is much kinder to your clothes. It's gentle on colored items, too. Alternatively, add one part baking soda and one part freshly squeezed lemon juice to your whites wash to get clothes really clean.

Appearance

It is amazing that something as inexpensive as

baking soda can be a boon to everyone who cares about appearance,

without having to pay a fortune. Baking soda can be used in so many

different ways to improve appearance, from alleviating irritating little rashes

to making your skin so healthy-looking that people will believe you

have used one of the luxury brands. Baking soda is so versatile

you can use it on most parts of your body.

Skin

Soothe Allergic Skin

If you are allergic to anything at all, from food to medication, more often than not the symptoms will show up on the skin in the form of a rash. These skin allergies can often take the shape of unsightly hives, which are very itchy and can take ages to disappear.

Although baking soda cannot help with curing the allergy, using it in your bathwater can bring enormous relief from the itching. Two cupfuls in a cool bath should be enough to relieve the symptoms, but if you find that particular areas of the body are causing you more intense discomfort, then undiluted baking soda can be rubbed into these areas for even more relief.

Ease Sunburn and Windburn

In much the same way as baking soda brings relief from allergic skin reactions, 400 g/14 oz/2 cups of

baking soda can also be added to a cool bath if you have a sunburn or have been out in a strong wind for too long. It will help take the burn out of the skin, but obviously it cannot remedy any other symptoms of too much sun that you might be experiencing.

If you've been on a boat and got windburn on your face the baking soda will soon soothe your skin.

 CAUTION: Remember that everyone's skin is different. Please be aware that these tips do not replace the advice of your doctor or beauty professional and, although baking soda is mild and natural, particular care should still be taken with sensitive skin. When using any new product, it is advisable to do a patch test before using on large areas.

Deal with Chickenpox Spots

If you cast your mind back to when you were a child and had those awful childhood illnesses, you may well remember how uncomfortable chickenpox was. There was the constant itching and the constant rebukes from your parents that you would scar yourself if you scratched the spots.

Well, if you ever come into contact with some poor soul who is experiencing similar problems, suggest that they make a paste of baking soda

and a little cool water. This can be applied directly to the spots without any fear of additional irritation. The paste will soothe the itching and make the patient feel much more comfortable

Relieve Insect Bites and Stings

How annoying is it when those nasty little bugs creep up on you and give you such a bite that you feel as if a lion has mauled you? The worst ones are those mosquitoes, which you can only hear and not see. These insect bites, or stings from wasps, are so itchy that sometimes you cannot sleep for wanting to scratch. And you know it is best not to touch them.

If you mix some baking soda into a paste with a little water and then smear it over the bite or sting, you will be amazed at how quickly it gives you relief from the itching.

Help Acne

In a similar way to the relief of the itching of chickenpox spots, baking soda can be used to relieve acne, which can also be very itchy. The baking soda is again mixed with a little cool, but not cold, water into a paste. The paste should be

applied to the affected area and left to dry for 5–10 minutes. The paste will relieve the irritation of the acne spots and will also act as an extremely mild and nonintrusive facial scrub. It will wash away easily from the face with cool water without damaging the skin in any other way.

Ease Razor Burn

When we talk about razor burn we automatically think of men shaving their face. But you can get razor burn on your legs or under your armpits, too, and that really can be just as uncomfortable for women as facial razor burn is for men. Once again a baking soda paste can come to the rescue quite quickly. Make the paste quite a thin one and dab it onto the area affected by the razor burn to get almost immediate relief from the burning sensation.

However, if that doesn't work quite as quickly as you would like, then you can sprinkle undiluted baking soda onto the skin

Exfoliate

Mixing a paste of three parts baking soda to one part water is a really great way of exfoliating the body's skin. It is also really inexpensive and easy to use.

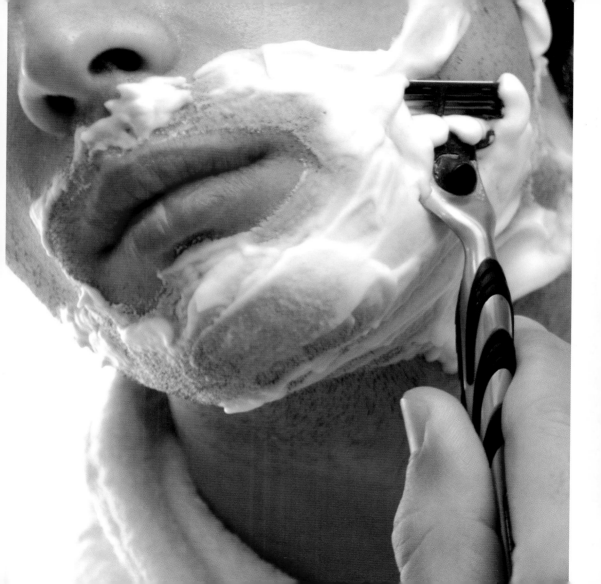

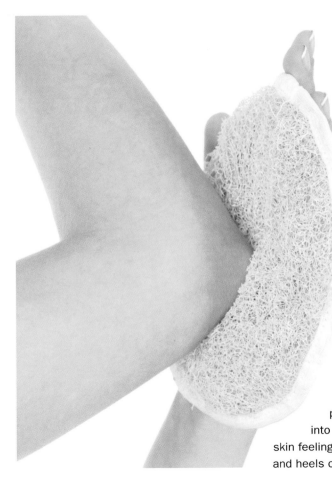

Facial Scrub

The same quantities used for exfoliation can be mixed to a paste and applied to the face as a facial scrub. Use it after washing for that freshly scrubbed feeling. Apply the facial scrub in a circular movement to the face and then rinse it off with cool water.

Rough Patches

Those little parts of your body that seem to acquire hard skin for no particular reason, for example the elbows and knees, will definitely benefit from a baking soda paste. Mix to a paste and rub into the affected area to leave the skin feeling softer. It works on the soles and heels of the feet as well.

Pen Stains on Fingertips

You know when an ink, ballpoint, or felt-tip pen decides to leak all over your fingers? Well, an easy way to remove this type of stain is to rub your hands together with a mix of baking soda and water. Rub away at the stain with confidence that it will not affect your skin but it will remove the stain. It will also remove some paint stains.

Hand Moisturizer

The tagline from one advertisement went "Now hands that do dishes can feel as soft as your face." Well that can be true of any dishpan red hands if you add a little baking soda into your dishwater. The baking soda softens your hands, no matter how long you have to stand at the kitchen sink.

Baking Soda Bath Salts

Lying in a hot bath when your body is aching from exertion must be one of the nicest feelings. But you don't have to pay expensive prices to buy salts to add to the bath. Mix equal quantities of sea salt and baking soda (about 200 g/7 oz/1 cup is fine for one bath) and 250 ml/8 fl oz/1 cup of the shampoo of your choice while the water is running.

Once the bath is halfway full, add your mixture and then fill the bath up with more water. You'll get some bubbles if you swirl your hand around and then you can soak to your heart's content.

Baking Soda Bath Oil

Making bath oil out of baking soda is just as easy as making bath salts, but this time you should let the bath fill completely before adding the mixture. Use the following ingredients and mix them in advance of your bath time.

In a mixing bowl add 225 g/8 oz/1 cup sea salt, 4 tablespoons baking soda, 250 ml/8 fl oz/1 cup honey, and 450 ml/16 fl oz/2 cups milk. Once the bath is full, pour the mixture in and add 115 ml/4 fl oz/½ cup of any of your favorite baby oil. This will give your skin a wonderful soft and silky feel and you are sure to feel nicely relaxed, too.

 CAUTION: Do not attempt to keep any over for the next bath—they have to be used fresh.

Dry Skin Bath Additive

If you have dry skin during the winter or because of an allergy, you can relieve it by mixing 100 g/3½ oz/½ cup baking soda, 75 g/3 oz/1 cup rolled oats, 250 ml/8 fl oz/1 cup warm water, and 1 tablespoon vanilla extract (or your favorite) into a paste. Add the mixture under the faucet while you are running your bath. It certainly stops the itching.

Hair

Conditioning the Hair

Sometimes if you use the same shampoo or mousse all the time, you can get a buildup on your hair, making it feel lank, greasy, drab, and lifeless. By adding 2 teaspoons baking soda to a teaspoon of your favorite shampoo and mixing them together you can help to condition your hair and remove the buildup. You just have to wash and then rinse your hair as normal with your mixture. This mix gives your hair a good shine and leaves it feeling really clean.

Hairbrushes and Combs

How embarrassing is it when someone asks you if they can borrow one of your hairbrushes or combs and they look absolutely filthy, or even if they are visible when visitors appear at your home? It can't be avoided easily because of hair, dirt, and grime, but why not try boiling them (if they are of a suitable material) for about 10 minutes in water and baking soda? Just add 200 g/7 oz/1 cup baking soda to the water and boil the dirt and grime away.

Teeth & Mouth

Whitening Teeth and Stain Removal

We all know that some of the commercial brands of whitening toothpastes contain baking soda. But you can use a little baking soda once a week on your wet toothbrush to do much the same thing. Just dip your wet toothbrush into a little baking soda and brush your teeth as normal. The baking soda also helps remove any stubborn stains from your teeth. You should not swallow this paste and only use it if there are no signs of rawness on your gums.

For badly stained teeth, you could add a little hydrogen peroxide, although this should be used with care and definitely not swallowed.

Plaque Removal

We all know how quickly plaque and tartar build up on the teeth and how much better

the teeth feel when the dentist has cleaned them. Using baking soda mixed with iodised salt on a wet toothbrush can help keep the plaque down.

Customized Toothpaste

If you like the taste of your regular toothpaste, then why not add some baking soda to it? By mixing the two together and placing the mixture into a sealed container, the mix will keep for ages. It will help keep down the plaque, as well as the stains, and keep your teeth whiter at the same time.

Cleaning Toothbrushes

We all do it—we grab the toothbrush without really giving any thought to the germs or bacteria that might be hiding on it. We brush away innocently. But the toothbrush can retain any number of germs and bacteria. To kill them, you can soak

your toothbrush in a weak paste made of baking soda and water mixed together. The toothbrush would be fine soaking all night and at least you would have peace of mind that it is clean when you are ready to use it the next morning.

Breath Freshener

You can make your own breath freshener —particularly useful if you dined on onions or garlic the night before! Using a gargle made of ½ teaspoon baking soda mixed with water could be part of your daily routine. This mix can kill off any germs and leave your mouth feeling much fresher.

When you really feel as if you should hide away from the world because of lingering breath odor, use ⅛ teaspoon baking soda mixed with some water to create your own instant breath freshener. Swish it around like a mouthwash and it will neutralize the lingering bad odors.

Cleaning on the Move

Wherever you are, if you are expecting to get close or speak to people, it is always nice to feel confident that your mouth is fresh. If you are off to a meeting or a hot date, then dipping a piece of chewing gum into water and then into a small amount of baking soda can

really help to make your mouth feel fresh and clean. Might be worth keeping a small container of it in your handbag or in the glove compartment of your car, just in case?

Nasty Cold Sores

Don't you just hate them? One minute you are just fine and then this huge, ugly, and unsightly "thing" appears on your lip. Don't panic though; You can treat a cold sore with some baking soda mixed with a little water. Gently—and we mean gently—rub the sore. You will feel relief and it will speed up the healing process.

 CAUTION: The cold-sore virus can be carried on your toothbrush, so remember to soak that in baking soda too.

Retainers and Dentures

Braces, retainers, and dentures can be soaked overnight in a mixture of baking soda and water. This mixture helps to kill off any germs that might have accumulated on them. It also helps to keep retainers looking bright and shiny. If dentures are badly stained, they can be scrubbed with a toothbrush that has been dipped in a baking soda paste.

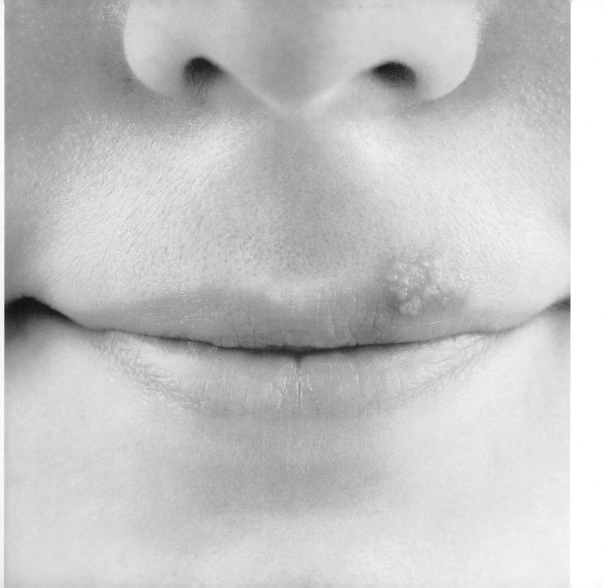

Odor & Feet

Smelly Feet

Smelly or itchy feet can really plague some people in the hot weather. But using baking soda as a talcum powder first thing in the morning can help keep the feet dry and itch-free all day. Use it before you put on your socks and footwear. Good for your feet and good for those around them, too

Underarm Deodorant

You can even use baking soda to make an underarm deodorant—how cool is that? Just mix together 4 teaspoons potassium alum (which you can buy in block form; it is used as an aftershave and rubbed over a freshly shaven face) with 2 teaspoons baking soda and 250 ml/8 fl oz/1 cup alcohol.

You can decant the mixture into a suitable plastic spray-capped bottle and it can be used daily. It keeps you fresh and dry all day long and the added bonus is that it does not contain any harmful chemicals.

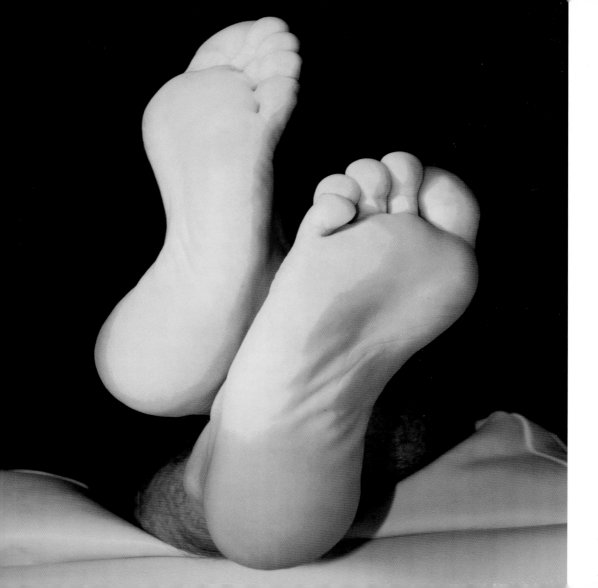

Body Odor

Adding 100 g/3½ oz/½ cup baking soda to the bathwater will help eliminate perspiration smells, as well as neutralizing acids and dispersing oil. If you use baking soda like a talcum powder and apply it to your body with a powder puff, then you will feel fresh all day long. You can use it all over to keep the odors at bay.

Hands

You have just finished preparing a beautiful meal and the guests are due to arrive.

You put your hands to your face, only to discover that they smell of garlic, onion, and any combination of different food smells. Don't worry though—a little baking soda used as soap with a little water will quickly neutralize the smells and make you feel much better.

If your hands are particularly dirty, you can mix one part of baking soda with three parts of either water or liquid hand wash to clean them up, then rinse off the grime. And don't forget to add some baking soda to the dishwater, too.

Talcum Powder

Baking soda straight from the package works just like a talcum powder if you sprinkle it on to your skin. The baking soda helps absorb any excess moisture, particularly when the temperature is high, it is a bit too humid, and you have been perspiring. Just like your favorite talcum powder, the baking soda makes you feel fresh all over.

Tired Feet

If you've been on your feet all day at work, or spent the day "shopping until you nearly dropped" then a footbath can feel wonderful. If you mix 200 g/7 oz/1 cup baking soda into some comfortably hot water, lower your feet gently in, and then relax, you'll be amazed how wonderful your feet feel afterward. And your feet will be softened, too!

Baby Care

Because baking soda is not harmful to children and babies,

it is the perfect way to keep the nursery clean and smelling fresh.

Baking soda can be used for many baby-related tasks. It can be used to

clean baby and his or her toys, as well as to eliminate those sometimes

overpowering baby smells around the home. You can use baking soda

with confidence around baby; it contains nothing that can irritate

the skin or cause any allergic reactions.

Bathing & Treatments

Baby Bath

Adding 200 g/7 oz/1 cup of baking soda to baby's bath can help keep his or her skin wonderfully soft. You can use it instead of a bubble bath and rest easy that it won't irritate the baby's skin.

Cleaning Bath Toys

Baby's bath toys can get a buildup of lime scale. To remove this, sprinkle some baking soda onto a damp cloth and scrub clean. The baking soda also eliminates any lingering smells on the toys. For really stubborn lime scale on the toys you could make a paste of baking soda and water and scrub with an old toothbrush.

Cradle Cap Treatment

To effectively remove what can be unsightly cradle cap, mix together some baking soda and water. Smear it onto the affected area about an hour before bath time, then rinse the mixture off in the bath.Adding some baking soda to olive oil is another cradle cap treatment. Mix the two together and apply to the affected area by smearing it on.

 CAUTION: It is quite messy, so use old sheets if you can.

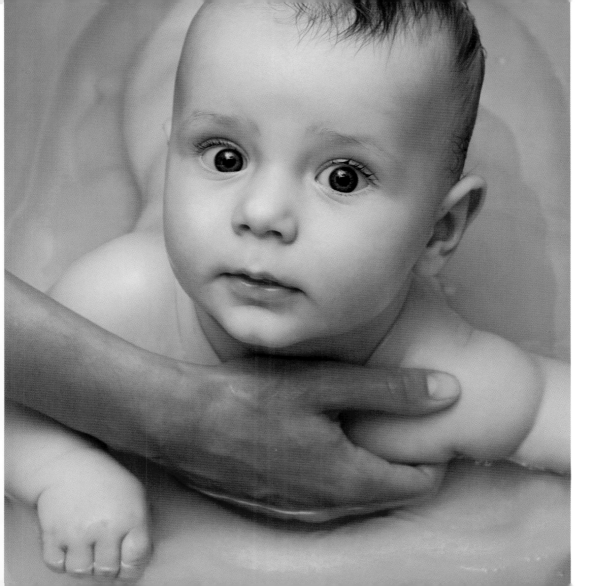

Diaper Rash Treatment

Diaper rash can be so uncomfortable for baby. If you've tried all the commercial brands and they've not worked, try putting 1–2 teaspoons baking soda in the bathwater after you've washed baby's face. The baking soda will soothe the baby's skin and help prevent diaper rash from coming back.

If the diaper rash is causing serious discomfort you can use baking soda at every diaper change. Dissolve 1 teaspoon in 250 ml/8 fl oz/1 cup warm water and apply it to the baby's bottom. Apply around the whole of the affected area and let the mixture air-dry naturally.

Thrush in the Mouth Treatment

If your baby is experiencing thrush in the mouth, which is common in infants, mix together ¼ teaspoon baking soda, 250 ml/8 fl oz/1 cup water, and a drop of liquid soap. Using a spotlessly clean cotton cloth, dab the mixture onto the baby's tongue 4–6 times a day. It won't hurt baby.

Cleaning & Odor Removal

Crib and Playpen

Because baking soda is not harmful to children or babies, it can be used to freshen up their room. It deodorizes smells and leaves the whole room smelling fresh.

Babies' cribs can often get grimy, particularly when they start pulling themselves up. To get rid of finger marks and grease, use a mixture of 100 g/ 3½ oz/½ cup baking soda, 50 ml/ 2 fl oz/¼ cup distilled white vinegar, and 2.25 L/4 pts/2¼ qts warm water. This mixture will get rid of smells in the crib, too.

Any urine smells lingering in the nursery or child's room can be eliminated by sprinkling some baking soda on to the mattress of the crib or the bed when changing the sheets.

The playpen can get just as mucky, if not more so, than the crib. And the playpen often has lingering food, vomit, and urine smells. Use the same mixture as for cleaning the crib. This will deodorize the playpen and make it a nicer place for baby to play.

Bottles

Put a couple of tablespoons of baking soda in baby's bottles and fill them with water. Let them soak overnight and the sour smells will disappear.

If your baby's bottles can be put in the dishwasher, add some baking soda to the powder or tablet area. This will ensure that the dishwasher is clean enough to wash the baby's bottles

Teats and Pacifiers

When teats and pacifiers are not in use they can be kept in cold water to which a pinch of baking soda has been added.

 CAUTION: Rinse well afterward.

Teats and pacifiers can get discolored and stained, particularly when the baby has moved on to solid foods. To remove the stains, mix a weak paste of baking soda and water, and give them a good scrub.

Toy Box

You can clean baby's toy box, too. Once a month mix together 200 g/7 oz/1 cup baking soda with an equal quantity of distilled white vinegar. Use the mixture to clean the toy box and wipe all toys made of suitable material.

Cuddly Toys

Baking soda works on soft cuddly toys just as well. Put them in a clean pillowcase and add some baking soda, which you should sprinkle over the toys. If you give them a good shake, they'll come out smelling as fresh as daisies.

Crayon Marks

It is going to happen as your baby starts to get mobile—crayon on the walls and paintwork. Mix up a paste of baking soda soda and water. With an old toothbrush apply the paste to the mark—magic, it's gone

Washing Cloth Diapers

Some babies can develop an allergy to laundry powder that can cause diaper rash. Try putting 200 g/7 oz/1 cup of baking soda in the wash to help avoid this.

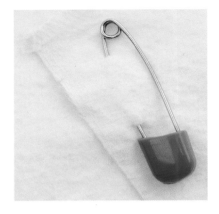

The laundry powder you use regularly can build up on diapers and baby clothes over time. To eliminate the buildup of laundry powder, replace it for one wash with 200 g/7 oz/1 cup of baking soda. Use similar quantities to your laundry powder. It won't lather so much but it will reduce the buildup.

You can keep your diapers looking bright and white if you add 100 g/3½ oz/1/2 cup baking soda to your washing machine. Put it in the powder chamber of your machine and you'll be proud to hang those white diapers out to dry

Diaper Pail

If you use terry or cloth diapers, the diaper pail will inevitably get smelly. Sprinkle some baking soda (about 200 g/7 oz/1 cup) over each diaper as you add it to the pail. This will deodorize the smells until laundry day.

Deodorizing Clothes

To eliminate baby smells from their clothes, and from your own, add 100 g/3½ oz/½ cup baking soda to water and soak the clothes for a few hours before washing.

If the baby's clothes don't need a wash, but just need to be freshened up, you can sprinkle them with some baking soda to deodorize any lingering odors. Let them sit overnight if you can, and the stale smells will be gone by the morning.

Health

Baking soda is so safe to use that you can also ingest it.

Although it is artificially produced for mass use, it is a compound that

also occurs naturally as sedimentary mineral deposits; it is not the usual

horrible synthetic chemicals that we often wash down the drain, so it is not

harmful to us or to the environment as a whole. That's why it is so good

to use as a healthcare product. The other added advantage is that it is

cheap to buy and readily available in varying quantities.

Feel Better

Energy Drink

A really inexpensive and effective energy drink for all the family can be made by adding baking soda to a sugar-free children's drink. Mix 1 teaspoon baking soda, 1 tablespoon salt, 5 teaspoons sugar, and 2.25 L/4 pts/2¼ qts water with the sugar-free drink and refrigerate it. It keeps for a while.

Your baking soda energy drink can be used in exactly the same way as any commercial energy drink. Pour it into a reusable bottle and it can go anywhere with you or the children. It must be better for them than those fizzy, sugary drinks you can buy and it's cheaper!

Itchy Eyes

If you are experiencing itchy eyes that could be the result of an allergy to pollen, you can soothe them with baking soda eyewash. Add ½ teaspoon baking soda to half a glass of water and bathe the eyes with an eyebath. The mixture will keep in the refrigerator for a couple of days.

Contact Lenses

Daily wear contact lenses need cleaning every day. Add a pinch of baking soda to your cleaner to make it mildly abrasive. This helps prevent buildup and could extend the life of the lenses.

Reaction to Poison Ivy

Ever touched poison ivy by mistake and wished you never had? Really itchy, isn't it? You can deal with the resulting rash by soaking in a bath containing 100 g/3½ oz/½ cup baking soda.

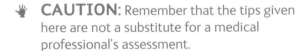 **CAUTION:** Remember that the tips given here are not a substitute for a medical professional's assessment.

Stuffy Nose

All blocked up? Using baking soda in a vaporizer can really help to clear a stuffy nose quickly. Fill the vaporizer with water to the indicated level, then add and stir in 1 teaspoon salt and 1 teaspoon baking soda until they are dissolved. Now breathe in the vapor to clear the congestion.

This is a really good tip for those who cannot or do not want to use store-bought decongestants. Pregnant women, children, and those who have medical conditions are often prevented from using medication. Baking soda is a safe alternative for everyone, whatever their circumstances.

Not only does baking soda in your vaporizer help clear your stuffy nose and reduce the symptoms of a cold, but it also deodorizes your house and removes lingering odors. How's that for a good bargain?

Fever Reduction

If one of your loved ones has a high fever, there's nothing quite as effective and speedy to reduce the temperature as a baking soda bath. Add some baking soda to a cool, but not cold, bath and the temperature will plummet fast.

Children's high temperatures will really drop quickly if you put them into the cool baking soda bath. They will feel much more comfortable. Of course, the added bonus is that it washes them squeaky clean at the same time as lowering their temperature.

Indigestion

Baking soda is known to be an effective antacid, so it can work for most stomach discomforts, particularly things such as indigestion and heartburn, which can make you feel really uncomfortable.

If you are one of those unfortunate people who regularly suffer from that bloated feeling after a meal, try sprinkling a little baking soda on to your food. It helps to reduce the buildup of gas that causes the bloated feeling. You can use baking soda whenever you've got excessive bloating for whatever reason.

Some foods and drinks can give you heartburn every time you eat or drink them. But you don't have to suffer in silence or give up consuming them. Add 1 teaspoon baking soda to a glass of water and the burning feeling will disappear really quickly.

Other types of food, perhaps those that are greasy or really rich, can give you an upset stomach. This is particularly true if you don't make a habit of eating a good old eggs and bacon breakfast. When you do, try adding 1 teaspoon baking soda to your glass of water and your stomach soon settles down.

Outside & Maintenance

Yard & Do-It-Yourself

Probably the most fundamental reason for using baking soda

in the yard and areas outside of your house is the cost. Baking soda

is so cheap that needing large quantities of it to complete the job is not

a problem. In addition, because baking soda is a natural product, the fact

that you are using large amounts outside does not pose a threat to

the environment. There are so many useful outside jobs

you can do with it you'll be amazed.

Tools & Equipment

Preserve those Tools

Shovels, spades, rakes – indeed all your garden tools – should be put away for the winter in a clean state to help preserve them. You can make a thick paste with baking soda and distilled white vinegar to give them a good clean. This will also stop rust forming over the winter months.

Polished Pots

If your flowerpots are not frost-resistant, then they should also be stored away before winter in cold regions. But if you put them away dirty, you will find yourself faced with twice the job of cleaning them in the spring. Use a baking soda and distilled white vinegar paste to clean them and then wash it off with some hot, soapy water. They'll sparkle in the spring!

Potato Trick

If any of your garden tools have been neglected and become rusty, you can use a potato and some baking soda to renew them. Just peel the potato and keep dipping it in the baking soda and rub until the rust has all been removed from the metal tool. Shiny again

Happy Pots

If you line your terra-cotta flowerpots with a thin layer of baking soda before filling them with soil, it will help to keep the soil fresh. It will kill any lingering bacteria and germs that may have remained from the last plants.

Outdoor Furniture & Surfaces

Wash that Plastic

Garden furniture is not cheap, so if you want to prolong its life you have to take care of it. Plastic garden furniture should be washed before it is put into storage for the winter. Add 200 g/7 oz/1 cup baking soda to some hot soapy water and wash the furniture with the mix. This will help remove stains, too.

Bright Whites

If your garden furniture is all white in color, you can keep it that way by adding some lemon juice to your baking soda mix. Squeeze the lemon juice into your hot water and baking soda mix. It is as good as bleaching the white furniture.

Clean the Barbecue

Cleaning the barbecue can be a tiresome job and also a messy one. But to clean the appliance without causing any scratching to the stainless steel surface, try sprinkling some baking soda straight onto a damp brush. Coat the barbecue well with the baking soda, give it a good scrub, then rinse clean.

Secure Repairs

Do you have any repairs that need doing on your garden furniture? If the furniture is plastic and you intend to use superglue, you can make the repair even stronger by adding a little baking soda to the glue. Sprinkle the baking soda onto the superglue while it is still wet.

Pool Perfection

While you're busy cleaning the yard in general, the children's paddling pool might benefit from a bit of tender loving care, too. Get rid of any mold or mildew by rubbing it inside and out with a mix of water, baking soda, and distilled white vinegar. Good as new and safe for the children next year.

Birdbaths

Even the birdbath needs a good clean from time to time, but don't worry about harming the creatures that drink from it or bathe in it. Using baking soda and water mixed to a paste will remove all stubborn grime and won't affect the birds at all.

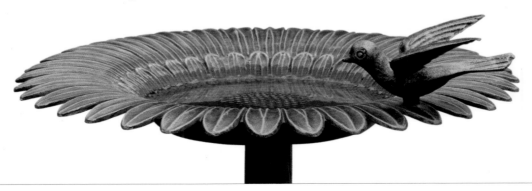

Walkways, Patios and Decking

Although it might take a whole box of baking soda to clean your walkways and patio areas, it is still effective and inexpensive. Wet the baking soda a little bit after you've sprinkled it over your concrete areas and then scrub with a stiff outdoor broom to remove stains and moss from the concrete.

You could use the sprinkling and brushing technique for cleaning your wooden decking too. Sprinkle the baking soda on and brush with a dry broom, but wash away the dirt and grime with water afterwards.

Hygienic Hammocks

Outdoor hammocks can be wiped down with a baking soda and water mix. This will get rid of any built-up grime and also bring out their color, not to mention making them smell really fresh for you, too, when you swing next summer.

Cleaner and Safer Toys

Children's outdoor toys, such as trampolines or slides and seesaws, as well as plastic cars and scooters, all need the baking soda touch. Baking soda mixed with water will bring the colors back to life and keep the dust levels at a minimum. Must be better and healthier for the children to use clean toys in the yard?

Plastic outdoor toys can become brittle if they are stored away in a warm environment during the winter months. To counteract this effect you can wipe the toys with a mixture of baking soda and distilled white vinegar. The two ingredients, when mixed together, will clean and protect the toys at the same time.

Snow and Ice

Baking soda acts very much like salt on snow and ice. Because the baking soda, like salt, freezes at a lower temperature than water, it is an ideal way to melt snow once it has covered your concrete. Sprinkle it over freshly fallen snow to help it melt quickly. Then add some more in case the slush freezes.

For a more preventive measure, if snow and ice are forecast, you can stop the water from freezing overnight by sprinkling baking soda onto your concrete. Use it on your walkways and steps in the yard to stop falls and accidents. Sprinkle it generously and cover as much of the concrete as you can.

Greenhouses & Plants

Wash Down

Some people use a store-bought cleaner to clean their greenhouses in the fall. However, if you want an ingredient that is just as effective, but cheaper, you can use baking soda. Wash all the surfaces, including the roof and walls, with baking soda and water. It will kill any mold and bacteria that may have formed during the growing season, as well as make the glass shine.

For an alternative mixture to wipe down the surfaces in your greenhouse and remove dirt and grime, mix 4 teaspoons baking soda with 120 ml/4 fl oz/½ cup distilled white vinegar and 2.25 L/4 pts/ 2¼ qts water. You can even put this mixture into a spray bottle, bit by bit, to make it easier to apply. Simply wipe off the dirt with a damp cloth.

Greenhouse Fungicide

Baking soda has been used for years as a mild fungicide,

particularly by organic growers. It can be used against powdery mildew and other plant diseases in the greenhouse, too. Mix 5 tablespoons baking soda with 4 L/7 pts/4 qts water and spray the greenhouse and the affected plants.

Routine for Roses

No matter how careful a gardener you are, mold and mildew still spread really quickly once they take hold. To keep mold on plants, particularly roses, at bay, you can spray with a mixture of 200 g/7 oz/1 cup baking soda and 2.25 L/ 4 pts/2¼ qts water. It certainly stops the mold from spreading to other plants.

Clean the Bottle

When you've sprayed your garden plants, be sure to kill any mildew or fungus inside the spray nozzle. Add a little baking soda and this should do the job for you. Also, before you put your sprayer into storage, do the same thing so it's fresh when watering time comes around again.

 CAUTION: You will have to fill the spray several times, but do make sure you cover all the diseased parts of the plant, including the foliage.

Defeat Disease

You can mix 4 teaspoons baking soda into 7.5 L/11¾ pts/2 gal water to treat diseased plants.
Apply the mixture generously to the diseased plants with a handheld spray.

Free the Lawn
from Mold

If your lawn needs some serious attention, there's no better way to give it a boost than baking soda, particularly if you have problems with mold. Use 1 tablespoon to 4 L/7 pts/1 gal water and spray the lawn, or you can apply it with a watering can. It kills off mold or mildew without having to use a fungicide and gives the lawn a bit of a tonic.

Another way of spreading the baking soda onto your lawn is to fill a sock or an old pair of tights with some undiluted baking soda. Beat the side of the sock or the tights with your hands to

release the dust. You get more of an even spread this way and you can always water it in with a hose if it doesn't rain.

Acid or Alkaline?

You can test the acidity of your soil by adding a pinch of baking soda to 1 tablespoon of your soil. If the mixture fizzes, the soil's pH is probably low and could do with a weak solution of baking soda and water. This mixture will help plants, such as geraniums, begonias, and hydrangeas, to bloom. They like a more alkaline soil.

Sweeter Tomatoes

Tomato plants like baking soda, too! Sprinkle a little around their roots regularly from the first planting. The baking soda will reduce their acidity and make them even sweeter to eat.

Blooming Marvellous

After cutting flowers from the garden to take into the house, why not try dipping their stems in a mild baking soda and water mix? It will help the flowers to stay fresh longer and kills any bacteria on the stems.

Pest Control

Ants No More!

Ants—whoever needs them? Although they don't do much damage they are still off-putting, particularly if they are near your doors and windows. You can sprinkle undiluted baking soda around their entrance and exit areas to help get rid of them and hopefully stop them getting into the house.

Ants also seem to love children's sandboxes. If they are invading your child's sandbox, then mix a whole container of baking soda well into the sand. That should keep them away.

Fleeing Fleas

Fleas don't like baking soda either. You can sprinkle it on your lawn, where they often congregate, believe it or not. Or you can sprinkle the baking soda directly onto your pet to make sure they don't stay on too long either.

Clear out Cockroaches

Cockroaches seem to like damp places and places where water congregates. You don't want cockroaches in your home because they spread so many germs. Try and keep damp areas free of the little devils, particularly around water pipes and in basements, by sprinkling neat baking soda in these areas.

Repel Rabbits

No matter how sweet we think they are, rabbits can do a lot of damage in the garden. They can be particularly harmful to plants that have been recently planted and especially to lettuce and cabbage. To ward off rabbits, sprinkle some baking soda generously around the vegetable garden.

Say No to Slugs and Snails

Slugs and snails can do even more damage than rabbits. They can destroy a newly planted vegetable or bedding plant overnight by eating the sweet leaves. At least if you use the baking soda generously, you should be able to deter most of these pests in one fell swoop. And your plants might actually feed you.

Painting & Decorating

Soften Paintbrushes

If you've been really bad and not cleaned your paintbrushes properly the last time you used them, there is an overnight remedy. Mix together 200 g/7 oz/1 cup baking soda, 60 ml/2 fl oz/ ¼ cup distilled white vinegar, and 2.25 L/4 pts/2¼ qts hot water. Soak the brushes in the mixture overnight and by morning they should be soft and ready to use.

Sticky Residue Remover

When you have painted a window, to remove any glue left from masking tape, simply make a paste of baking soda and water. Rub gently with the paste to remove the glue residue.

You can use the same mix of baking soda and water to remove poster glue from windows. If you've been advertising a local event and there is some glue residue on the window, use this mix to remove it completely and easily.

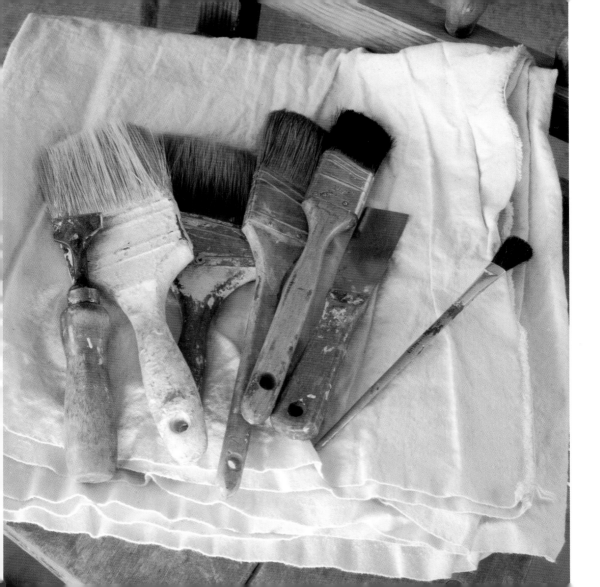

Wash Down Walls

To keep your outside walls clean and bright, you can wash them down with a mixture of 100 g/3½ oz/ ½ cup baking soda to each 4 L/7 pts/1 gal water. It will clean efficiently and bring colors back to almost new. The mix can be used on most outside wall materials.

You can use the same mixture (100 g/3½ oz/½ cup baking soda to each 4 L/7 pts/1 gal water) to wash down your walls and paintwork before you begin to repaint them. This mixture will remove all the dirt and grime, as well as any of the old paint that may be flaking.

Stripping Wallpaper

If you are planning to strip wallpaper, you can make the job much easier if you add 1 tablespoon baking soda to the water. Stir it in until it has dissolved and then wet the walls ready for stripping in the normal way. Let is soak in well and you'll be amazed how much easier the paper comes off.

Vehicles

Cars, bikes, and motorcycles can be messy. Let's face it, we spend so much time in our vehicles that it isn't surprising that sometimes they are our pride and joy and at others they are the bane of our lives. If we aren't worrying about cleaning them, then we're worrying about selling them. Keeping them in tip-top condition can only be good when it comes to getting a good price for "her." Being safe when we're working on our cars and bikes is so vitally important. Baking soda can help with all these things.

Cars & Bikes

Oil and Gas Spills

If you've got a car that leaks oil or gasoline on the floor of your garage then you might like to try the baking soda remedy for removing the stain. You just need to sprinkle a mixture of baking soda and salt over the spill. Let it soak for a while to absorb all the oil or gasoline. Then all you need to do is sweep the floor.

Even if the oil or gasoline leaks onto your driveway, baking soda and salt will still lift the stain efficiently.

 CAUTION: Give the mix plenty of time to soak up all the liquid up before you sweep the drive.

Odor Removal

If the car has not been used for some time, it can begin to smell musty inside. Neutralize these smells by sprinkling baking soda all-around. You can put it in the trunk, on the seat, and on the mats without any fear of damaging the interior upholstery.

Got smelly ashtrays in your car? You can get rid of that lingering smell by putting 100 g/3½ oz/½ cup baking soda into the ashtray when it is clean. The baking soda will neutralize the smell of the smoke and leave the whole car deodorized and smelling fresher.

Extinguishing Fires

Small fires can be extinguished in a garage or workshop using baking soda. Pour a complete container of the baking soda onto the fire and it will extinguish it. It's a good idea to keep some on the shelf just in case, particularly if you regularly use a flame in the garage or workshop.

You could also keep some baking soda in the trunk of your car. It is particularly effective at extinguishing electrical fires. The baking soda smothers the fire and brings its temperature down quite quickly.

 CAUTION: Baking soda should not be applied to fires in deep fryers as it may cause the grease to splatter.

Bugs on Bikes

To remove bugs that may have got stuck to the side mirrors of your bicycle or motorcycle, you can wash them with a mixture of baking soda and water. The bugs will come off quite easily, but you won't scratch the mirror.

Rusty Bikes

Bicycles can go rusty quite quickly, particularly if they are housed in a garage or shed. Vinegar and baking soda mixed to a paste will give them a general clean, but if there are any rust patches developing, give them a particularly good scrub. The mix should remove the rust quite easily.

Soda Shine

To give the chrome on a bicycle or motorcycle an extra shine, apply a baking soda and water paste. Smear it onto the chrome and then let it dry naturally in the air. When it is dry, you can buff the chrome with a soft cloth and you'll be able to see your face in it.

Kids' Stuff

Fun Projects for Children

What a really fun and inexpensive play material baking soda can be. Your children will be safely amused for hours making clay, volcanoes, and rockets out of baking soda. The ingredients are all cheap and easy to get hold of and the added bonus is that there is nothing that can harm the children. What more could a busy parent ask for, particularly when the children are also learning useful science- and math-related stuff at the same time?

Clay

Your children will love making this easy-to-mold clay. It is safe to use and the ingredients are so cheap—certainly much less than most store-bought brands of clay. The children can add food coloring to it if they want at the very beginning of the project, or they can also decorate it with paint, felt-tip pens, or watercolor pens after they've formed their shapes. This recipe makes a good-size piece of baking soda clay.

You Will Need:

1 large container (400 g/16 oz/2 cups) baking soda
200 g/7 oz/1 cup cornstarch
250 ml/8 fl oz/1 cup water
1 tbsp vegetable oil

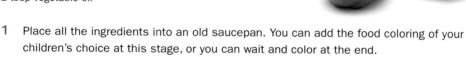

1   Place all the ingredients into an old saucepan. You can add the food coloring of your children's choice at this stage, or you can wait and color at the end.
2   Heat the mixture very slowly, stirring all the time until the mixture becomes thick and uniform in shape. The heating stage usually takes about 15 minutes or so on a low heat.
3   When the mixture is the right consistency, pour it out of the saucepan and onto an old plate.
4   Cover the clay with a damp cloth and let it cool for about an hour.
5   Once the clay has cooled enough to be handled, you can sprinkle some more cornstarch onto a wood board and knead the clay, as you would bread, until the clay is smooth.
6   Now you can let the children loose. The clay can be molded into any shape that your children want. They can also use their favorite colors to highlight the shapes. Felt-tip pens or watercolour pens are good for this important task.

Fizzy Sherbet

There is no cooking involved in making this fun fizzy treat for the children, but getting the taste right can be a case of trial and error. The sugar may have to be adjusted to give the right level of sweetness, which varies from person to person, and the same applies to the tartness or lemony-ness of the sherbet.

Science Made Fun

Making fizzy sherbet is a really good science-related project for the children. They will learn when you explain to them that the sugar and the citric acid give the sherbet the flavor.

You can also talk about carbon dioxide when you see that the citric acid and baking soda mixed together produce the fizzing action on the tongue. Remember that you only get the fizzing when the sherbet mixes with the saliva on the tongue.

Start With:

2 tsp superfine sugar or
confectioners' sugar

1 tsp powdered citric acid

½ tsp baking soda

1   Mix the ingredients together.
2   Test for sweetness and
    if necessary add some
    more sugar.
3   If the sherbet does not taste
    quite lemony enough, add
    some more citric acid.
4   If the sherbet isn't quite fizzy
    enough on your tongue, then
    add some more baking soda

You can also vary the flavor of
your sherbet when you've got this
initial ingredient mix just right. But
remember that all the ingredients have to be dry, otherwise the sherbet will fizz with any
liquid you add before it gets onto your tongue. You could try adding vanilla, coffee, cloves,
cinnamon, dry ginger powder, and a host of other dry ingredients.

There are various ways you can eat the sherbet—such as simply spooning it into your mouth
with a spoon or shovel-shape straw—but one of the most enjoyable for children is to dip a
lollipop or stick of liquorice into the sherbet.

Crunchy Toffee

Crunchy toffee, also known by some as "cinder toffee," is a really good fun project to make with the children. It is also good to eat as a special treat. Crunchy toffee is a flexible recipe, which means you can add ingredients to it to bring about any number of changes in taste.

You Will Need:

a little butter
1 tsp baking soda
150 g/5 oz/¾ cup sugar
4 tbsp honey or corn syrup

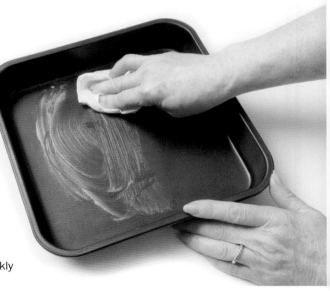

1   Lightly grease a baking tray with butter. Melt together the sugar and the honey or corn syrup over a low heat, stirring continuously to prevent burning, until they have caramelized.

2   Slowly add the teaspoonful of baking soda. Keep stirring continuously to prevent burning. As the baking soda hits the hot caramel it will bubble up very quickly and turn a burned orange color.

3   Once the mixture has stopped rising because of the baking soda, you can carefully remove it from the heat.

4   Pour the toffee mix onto the greased baking sheet and cover the hot mix with plastic wrap.

5   Once the toffee mix has cooled sufficiently, place in the refrigerator to harden.

6   Cut the crunchy toffee into bite-size squares to serve.

 CAUTION: Do not leave young children unattended around hot appliances.

Variations

Children's favorite flavorings, such as orange or strawberry, can be added to the toffee mix at the same time as the baking soda. Alternatively, or in addition to the flavorings, you can dip the set squares of toffee into melted dark, milk or white chocolate and leave to set before serving. You could even sprinkle chopped nuts or fruit-and-nut mix on the top of the still-wet chocolate if you want.

Inflate a Balloon

Showing children how to inflate a balloon using baking soda and vinegar is a really good science-related activity. The project gives them the chance to learn much about chemical reactions and the nature of solids, liquids, and gases.

When the baking soda and the vinegar you use in this activity are mixed together in your plastic bottle, they form carbon dioxide. As the carbon dioxide gas is made, pressure builds up inside the bottle so that the gas produced escapes into the balloon and inflates it.

You Will Need:
2 heaped tsp baking soda
150 ml/5 fl oz/⅔ cup vinegar
plastic drink bottle that can hold 600 ml/1pt/2½ cups
balloon
plastic funnel

1   Insert your plastic funnel into the neck of the balloon.
2   Spoon into the funnel your 2 heaped teaspoonfuls baking soda. Shake the baking soda so that it filters through the funnel and into the balloon.
3   Next, you need to pour your vinegar into the plastic bottle, again using your plastic funnel.
4   While holding the balloon tightly so that none of the baking soda falls out, you can now stretch the neck of the balloon over the neck of the plastic bottle.
5   Tip the balloon so that the baking soda falls into the vinegar and the two mix.

As the chemicals in the vinegar and the baking soda mix in the plastic bottle and give off fumes, your balloon will begin to inflate. Once the balloon has stopped inflating, you can remove it from the plastic bottle and tie the balloon in a knot as you would after the usual means of inflation.

Volcanic Eruption

This inexpensive project is a craft and science project. It takes time to organize, but is worth the effort; the kids will love it.

To Make the 'Volcano' Dough:

700 g/1½ lb/6 cups flour
350 g/12 oz/2 cups salt
4 tbsp vegetable oil
500 ml/18 fl oz/2 cups water

1   In a large bowl, mix all the dry ingredients together.
2   Add half the water and oil and knead to form a doughlike consistency.
3   Add the remaining water and oil gradually, working into a smooth and firm dough. If the mixture feels too dry, add more water.

To Create the Volcano:

plastic bottle that can hold 2 L/3½ pts/2 qts
2 heaped tsp baking soda
150 ml/5 fl oz/⅔ cup vinegar
2 l/3½ pts/2 qts warm water (continued overleaf)

few drops food coloring

few drops liquid soap

2 tbsp baking soda

baking sheet

1 Stand the clean, dry plastic bottle on your baking sheet and shape the dough around the bottle to form a volcano shape. Avoid dropping dough inside the bottle and leave the bottle opening free.

If time allows, let the volcano dry for two or three days before continuing. You could paint the volcano, providing the bottle opening and the inside of the bottle remain dry. However, if you can't wait to see the full effect of the volcano, you can make the lava right away:

2 Put a few drops of your chosen food coloring into the bottle.

3 Pour over the warm water until you have almost filled the bottle.

4 Add a few drops of liquid soap into the bottle.

5 Then add the baking soda to the soapy water in the bottle.

6 Now to make the lava explode! Just pour in your vinegar.

When the baking soda and vinegar mix together, they produce carbon dioxide gas. This bubbles up and forces your § lava to erupt.

Mini Rocket

The children will really enjoy this exciting and creative project.

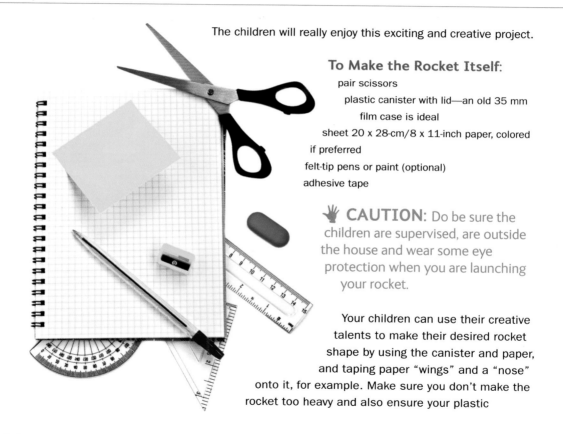

To Make the Rocket Itself:

pair scissors

plastic canister with lid—an old 35 mm film case is ideal

sheet 20 x 28-cm/8 x 11-inch paper, colored if preferred

felt-tip pens or paint (optional)

adhesive tape

CAUTION: Do be sure the children are supervised, are outside the house and wear some eye protection when you are launching your rocket.

Your children can use their creative talents to make their desired rocket shape by using the canister and paper, and taping paper "wings" and a "nose" onto it, for example. Make sure you don't make the rocket too heavy and also ensure your plastic

canister has a removable lid. You can make the rocket well in advance of launching it, particularly if the children want to paint or color their rocket. When you are ready to launch the rocket, it's time to make the rocket fuel.

To Make the Fuel:
½ tsp baking soda
½ tsp vinegar
tissue

You should not let your baking soda and vinegar mix until you are ready to launch the rocket. But when you are ready you can:

1   Wrap your baking soda in a tissue. Make a package that will easily fit inside the lid of your plastic canister.
2   Fix the baking soda package into the lid of the plastic canister with a little adhesive tape. Alternatively, make a paste with the baking soda and a little water and pack this into the lid.
3   Pour the vinegar into your plastic canister.
4   Carefully put the lid onto the canister, then turn the canister upside down so that the vinegar soaks through the tissue paper and mixes with the baking soda.

When the baking soda and the vinegar combine they will make carbon dioxide gas. This gas will force the plastic canister to pop off of the lid. The rocket will launch into the air, so stand back and enjoy!

Food

Culinary Tips

In addition to using baking soda in recipes, baking soda can also be used in a number of ways to prepare foodstuffs ready for cooking, or to preserve them for future use. Baking soda is a really useful and practical addition to any pantry shelf. It is cheap and inexpensive, and because it is not harmful to our bodies, you can use it to your heart's content. Baking soda is so versatile that it is amazing it does not carry a huge price tag.

Meat & Poultry

Free of Feathers

Sometimes when you buy a chicken there are a few feathers left on the skin. They won't do you any harm, but they can be a bit off-putting. To get rid of these quickly and easily, just rub the skin of the chicken with baking soda. Rinse the baking soda off before cooking the bird.

Tender Fowl

Baking soda is also really good for tenderizing chicken meat. Rub the meat liberally with some baking soda and then rinse it thoroughly for a really tender chicken.

Crispy Chicken

If you want the chicken skin to be crispy, you can rub in some baking soda before cooking. Crispy skin and tender meat—delicious!

Tone Down Flavor

You can use baking soda to reduce the strong flavor of meats such as venison, particularly if you are planning to preserve the meat. Add the baking soda to your preserving jar to get rid of an overwhelming flavor.

No Fowl Smell

If you are plucking and preparing your own chicken, you can get rid of the sometimes strong smell by sprinkling some baking soda into the cavity before drawing out the giblets.

Pork Crackling

If you like your pork crackling really crisp, then baking soda can do this for you. Sprinkle and smear some baking soda onto the pork skin before cooking. The baking soda will help the skin to turn crispy for you. Score the skin as usual, with crisscross cuts using a sharp knife. Cutting like this helps to crisp up the skin, too, and makes it easier to cut and share, because everyone will want some!

Smearing baking soda onto the skin of your pork meat will not only give you a crispy crackling, but it will also help keep the meat tender, too.

Marinade Me Tender

You can add ½ teaspoon baking soda to your meat marinade prior to cooking stir-fry dishes. The baking soda will help soften the texture of the meat, particularly if the meat you've bought is one of the tougher cuts. The meat will melt in your mouth.

Vegetables

Vibrant Carrots

Even if carrots are past their best, they can be rejuvenated by adding a little baking soda to the cooking water. Adding the baking soda has a double effect; it helps the color and helps keep them crisp, too.

White Cauliflower

Adding 2 tablespoons baking soda to the cooking water when you are boiling a cauliflower will help keep the flower of the vegetable nice and white.

Crisp Corn

If you want to keep your corn on the cob crisp, why not try adding 2 tablespoons baking soda to the cooking water

Soaking Beans

If you like to eat dried beans but want to soften them before cooking, you can help them along when soaking them overnight by adding 1 teaspoon baking soda to the water—with enough water to cover the beans completely.

Great Greens

To maintain the color of green vegetables you can add ½ teaspoon baking soda to the cooking water. This works really well for green beans, broccoli, and sprouts.

🖐 **CAUTION:** Do not forget that you should never overcook your greens—if you do, most of the goodness ends up in the water.

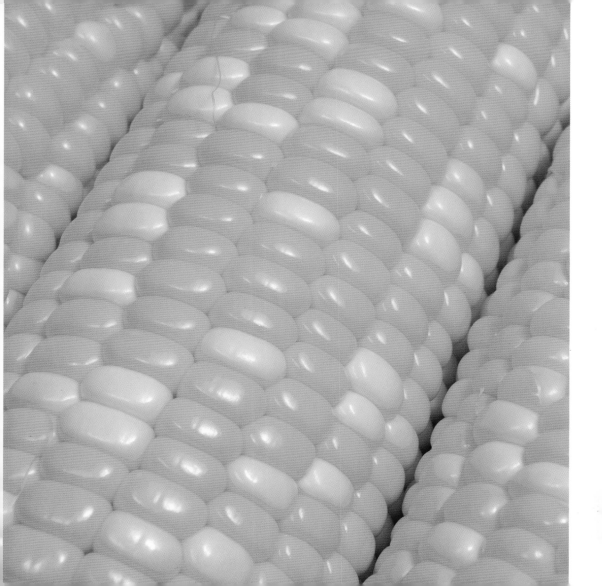

First-Class Cabbage

To reduce the cooking time of cabbage and to keep it tender, you just have to add 3 tablespoons baking soda to the cooking water. We all agree that there's nothing worse than overcooked cabbage!

Adding baking soda to your cabbage's cooking water can also help your family and friends avoid the ill effects of the vegetable's gasses after eating the meal. Must be much better for all concerned, we're sure you'll agree!

 CAUTION: Although baking soda has a positive visual effect on vegetables, don't be tempted to add too much or get into a habit of using it all the time, as it arguably can destroy the natural vitamins C and B1 in the veggies.

Speedy Tomatoes

If you are making your own tomato sauce or salsa, you can reduce the cooking time by adding some baking soda. Add 2 tablespoons baking soda for every 900 ml/1½ pts/1 qt cooking water. This can reduce the cooking time by at least 10 minutes.

Sweeter Tomatoes

Adding baking soda to the water you are cooking your tomatoes in when preparing your salsa or tomato sauce can also help to neutralize the acid in the tomatoes.

Milder Veg

In order to remove the harsher and stronger flavur from some wild vegetables, add around 1 teaspoon baking soda per 1 L/1¾ pts/1 qt water when you boil your vegetables. The color of the vegetables also becomes brighter.

Clean Veg

You can't be too careful when it comes to food handling and preparation. Wash your fruit and vegetables in cold water with 2–3 tablespoons baking soda added to it. This will help remove some of the impurities that our tap water leaves behind.

For more thorough cleaning, the dirt in or on your fruit and vegetables will wash away so much quicker and easier if you add 100 g/3½ oz/½ cup baking soda to the water.

To go further, if you want to be sure your store-bought vegetables are chemical-free when you cook them, try washing them with 200 g/7 oz/1 cup baking soda added to a sinkful of fresh water. More and more of the prepared vegetables and fruit look too good to be true—shiny fruit is often covered with edible wax, but baking soda will get rid of this for you.

Alternatively, you can dab a wet sponge or your vegetables brush into undiluted baking soda and use this to scrub your vegetables. The baking soda will remove the dirt, any wax, and pesticides. Give everything a thorough rinsing before serving or cooking your vegetables.

Other Uses

Baking Powder

Ever noticed how some recipes call for baking soda while others call for baking powder? As discussed in the Introduction, these are two different things. However, you can make your own baking powder by stirring and sifting together two parts cream of tartar to one part baking soda and one part cornstarch.

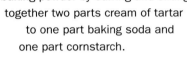 **CAUTION:** Resist the urge to add more baking soda or baking powder than a recipe instructs, as this can cause the food to taste bitter and it can also cause the bread or cake to rise too rapidly so that the air bubbles grow too large and burst, which in turn causes the mixture to collapse. On the other hand, too little baking powder or baking soda leads to a tough and densely textured product.

A Question of Taste

If you live in a hard-water area, perhaps you don't like the taste of your tap water? To improve the taste, you could add 1 teaspoon baking soda to each 2.25 L/4 pts/2¼ qts tap water.

Kitchen Cleaning

Don't forget to check out the section on kitchens (pages 14–45) for plenty of great tips on keeping your kitchen surfaces, appliances, and utensils in tip-top shape with baking soda.

Neutralize Acidity

If you experience stomach ulcers, it is important that you don't consume too much acid. There is plenty of citric acid in most fruit that can upset and inflame the stomach. You can neutralize the acid in coffee by adding 1 teaspoon baking soda to your cup or mug. Why not add it to the coffeepot when you make a fresh brew? Adding 2 or 3 teaspoons baking soda will be more than enough for everyone.

No More Beans Blues

You know how the saying goes, "beans, beans are good for your heart, the more you eat ..." Well, to solve the excess gas problem, try adding 1 teaspoon baking soda to your beans when you are cooking them. All of the bean goodness is there without the unpleasant aftereffects!

Recipes

Baking soda has been used throughout the ages as a raising agent in baking. This is its principal use in food, either used directly or as part of baking powder. If there is already some sort of acid in the recipe, then baking soda can be used, because it will react with the acid once a liquid is added, and then cause the carbon dioxide bubbles that enable the raising. Baking powder is used when there is no acid in the recipe.

Irish Soda Bread

Makes 1 loaf

400 g/14 oz/3¼ cups
white all-purpose flour,
plus 1 tbsp for dusting
1 tsp salt
2 tsp baking soda
15 g/½ oz/1 tbsp butter

50 g/2 oz/⅓ cup quick oats
1 tsp clear honey
2 tbsp milk
300 ml/½ pt/1¼ cups buttermilk

For a whole-wheat variation:

400 g/14 oz/3¼ cups
whole-wheat flour,
plus 1 tbsp for dusting
1 tbsp milk

1 Preheat the oven to 200°C/400°F, 15 minutes before baking. Sift the flour, salt, and baking soda into a large bowl. Rub in the butter until the mixture resembles fine bread crumbs. Stir in the oats and make a well in the center.

2 Mix the honey, buttermilk, and milk together and add to the dry ingredients. Mix to a soft dough.

3 Knead the dough on a lightly floured surface for 2–3 minutes, until the dough is smooth. Shape into a 20.5 cm/8 in round and place on an oiled baking sheet.

4 Thickly dust the top of the bread with flour. Using a sharp knife, cut a deep cross on top, going about halfway through the loaf.

5 Bake in the preheated oven on the middle shelf for 30–35 minutes or until the bread is slightly risen, golden, and sounds hollow when tapped underneath. Cool on a wire rack. Eat on the day of making.

6 For a whole-wheat soda bread, use all the whole-wheat flour instead of the white flour and add an extra tablespoon of milk when mixing together. Dust the top with whole-wheat flour and bake.

Cheese-crusted Potato Biscuits

Serves 4

200 g/7 oz/1¾ cups
    self-rising flour
3 tbsp whole-wheat flour
½ tsp salt
1½ tsp baking powder

25 g/1 oz/¼ stick butter, cubed
5 tbsp milk
175 g/6 oz/¼ cup cold
    mashed potato
freshly ground black pepper
2 tbsp milk, for brushing

40 g/1½ oz/6 tbsp mature
    Cheddar cheese,
    finely grated
paprika, to dust
basil sprig, to garnish

1 Preheat the oven to 220°C/425°F, 15 minutes before baking. Sift the flours, salt and baking powder into a large bowl. Rub in the butter until the mixture resembles fine breadcrumbs.

2 Stir 4 tablespoons of the milk into the mashed potatoes and season with black pepper.

3 Add the dry ingredients to the potato mixture, mixing together with a fork and adding the remaining 1 tablespoon of milk if needed.

4 Knead the dough on a lightly floured surface for a few seconds until smooth. Roll out to a 15 cm/6 inch round and transfer to an oiled baking sheet.

5 Mark the scone round into 6 wedges, cutting about halfway through with a small sharp knife.

6 Brush with milk, then sprinkle with the cheese and a faint dusting of paprika.

7 Bake on the middle shelf of the preheated oven for 15 minutes, or until well risen and golden brown.

8 Transfer to a wire rack and leave to cool for 5 minutes before breaking into wedges.

9 Serve warm or leave to cool completely. Once cool, store the biscuits in an airtight container. Garnish with a sprig of basil and serve split and buttered.

Fruity Apple Teabread

Cuts into 12 slices

125 g/4 oz/½ cup butter

125 g/4 oz/½ cup
light brown sugar

275 g/10 oz/2 cups
golden raisins

150 ml/¼ pint/⅔ cup apple juice

1 apple, peeled, cored,
and chopped

2 eggs, beaten

275 g/10 oz/2¼ cups
all-purpose flour

½ tsp ground cinnamon

½ tsp ground ginger

2 tsp baking soda

curls of butter, to serve

To decorate:

1 apple, cored and sliced

1 tsp lemon juice

1 tbsp corn syrup, warmed

1 Preheat the oven to 180°C/ 350°F. Oil and line the bottom of a 23 x 13 x 8-cm/ 9 x 5 x 3-inch loaf pan with nonstick parchment paper.

2 Put the butter, sugar, golden raisins, and apple juice in a small saucepan. Heat gently, stirring occasionally until the butter has melted. Turn into a bowl and let cool.

3 Stir in the chopped apple and beaten eggs. Sift the flour, spices, and baking soda over the apple mixture. Stir into the golden raisin mixture, spoon into the prepared loaf pan, and smooth the top level with the back of a spoon.

4 Toss the apple slices in lemon juice and arrange on top. Bake in the preheated oven for 50 minutes. Cover with aluminum foil to prevent the top from browning too much.

5 Bake for 30–35 minutes, or until a skewer inserted into the center comes out clean. Let stand in the pan for 10 minutes before turning out to cool onto a wire rack.

6 Brush the top with syrup and let cool. Remove the lining paper, cut into thick slices, and serve with curls of butter.

Carrot Cake

Cuts into 8 slices

200 g/7 oz/1⅔ cups
   all-purpose flour
½ tsp ground cinnamon
½ tsp freshly grated nutmeg
1 tsp baking powder
1 tsp baking soda
150 g/5 oz/⅔ cup
   dark brown sugar

200 ml/7 fl oz/¾ cup
   vegetable oil
3 eggs
225 g/8 oz/1¼ cups carrots,
   peeled and roughly grated
50 g/2 oz/½ cup
   chopped walnuts

For the icing:

175 g/6 oz/¾ cup cream cheese
finely grated rind of 1 orange
1 tbsp orange juice
1 tsp vanilla extract
125 g/4 oz/1 cup
   confectioners' sugar

1 Preheat the oven to 150°C/300°F 10 minutes before baking. Lightly oil and line the bottom of a 15-cm/6-inch deep square cake pan with nonstick parchment paper.
2 Sift the flour, spices, baking powder, and baking soda together into a large bowl. Stir in the brown sugar and mix together.
3 Lightly whisk the oil and eggs together, then gradually stir into the flour and sugar mixture. Stir well. Add the carrots and walnuts. Mix thoroughly, then pour into the prepared cake pan. Bake in the preheated oven for 1¼ hours, or until light and springy to the touch and a skewer inserted into the center of the cake comes out clean.
4 Remove from the oven and let cool in the pan for 5 minutes before turning out onto a wire rack. Reserve until cold.
5 To make the icing, beat together the cream cheese, orange rind, orange juice, and vanilla extract. Sift the confectioners' sugar and stir into the cream cheese mixture. When cold, discard the lining paper, spread the cream cheese icing over the top, and serve cut into squares.

Easy Chocolate Cake

Serves 8–10

75 g/3 oz dark chocolate,
    broken into squares
200 ml/7 fl oz/¾ cup milk
250 g/9 oz/1¼ cups dark
    muscovado/dark brown sugar
75 g/3 oz/⅓ cup (6 tbsp)
    butter, softened

2 large eggs, beaten
150 g/5 oz/1 heaped cup
    all-purpose flour
½ tsp vanilla extract
1 tsp baking soda
25 g/1 oz/¼ cup unsweetened
    cocoa powder

For the topping and filling:

125 g/4 oz/½ cup (1 stick)
    unsalted butter
225 g/8 oz/2¼ cups
    confectioners' sugar, sifted
8 large fresh strawberries, halved
tiny mint sprigs, to decorate

1 Preheat the oven to 180°C/350°F. Grease two 20.5 cm/8 inch round sandwich pans and line the bottoms with nonstick parchment paper.

2 Place the chocolate, milk and 75 g/3 oz/⅓ cup of the sugar in a heavy-based saucepan. Heat gently until the mixture has melted, then set aside to cool.

3 Place the butter and remaining sugar in a large bowl and whisk with an electric mixer until light and fluffy. Gradually whisk in the eggs, adding 1 teaspoon flour with each addition.

4 Stir in the cooled melted chocolate mixture along with the vanilla extract. Sift in the flour, baking soda, and cocoa powder, then fold into the mixture until smooth.

5 Spoon the batter into the pans and smooth level. Bake for about 30 minutes until a skewer inserted into the center comes out clean. Turn out to cool on a wire rack.

6 To decorate, beat the butter with the confectioners' sugar and 1 tablespoon warm water until light and fluffy, then place half in a piping bag fitted with a star nozzle.

7 Spread half the buttercream over one sponge layer and scatter half the strawberries over it. Top with the other cake and spread the remaining buttercream over the top. Pipe a border of stars around the edge. Decorate with the remaining strawberries and mint sprigs.

Honey Cake

Cuts into 6 slices

50 g/2 oz/¼ cup butter

2 tbsp superfine sugar

125 g/4 oz/⅓ cup clear honey

175 g/6 oz/1⅓ cups
    all-purpose flour

½ tsp baking soda

½ tsp pumpkin pie spice

1 large egg

2 tbsp milk

25 g/1 oz/¼ cup flaked almonds

1 tbsp clear honey, to drizzle

1 Preheat the oven to 180°C/350°F, 10 minutes before baking. Lightly oil and line the bottom of an 18 cm/7 inch deep round cake pan with lightly oiled waxed paper or parchment paper.

2 In a saucepan, gently heat the butter, sugar and honey until the butter has just melted.

3 Sift the flour, baking soda, and mixed spice together into a bowl.

4 Beat the egg and the milk until thoroughly mixed.

5 Make a well in the center of the sifted flour and pour in the melted butter and honey.

6 Using a wooden spoon, beat well, gradually drawing in the flour from the sides of the bowl.

7 When all the flour has been beaten in, add the egg mixture and mix thoroughly. Pour into the prepared pan and sprinkle with the flaked almonds.

8 Bake in the preheated oven for 30–35 minutes until well risen and golden brown and a skewer inserted into the center of the cake comes out clean.

9 Remove from the oven, cool for a few minutes in the pan before turning out and leaving to cool on a wire rack. Drizzle with the remaining tablespoon of honey and serve.

Chocolate Chip Cherry Muffins

Makes 12

75 g/3 oz/⅓ cup
candied cherries
75 g/3 oz/scant ½ cup
semisweet or dark
chocolate chips

75 g/3 oz/⅓ cup soft margarine
200 g/7 oz/1 cup
superfine sugar
2 large eggs
150 ml/¼ pint/⅔ cup thickset
natural yogurt

5 tbsp milk
275 g/10 oz/2 heaped cups
all-purpose flour
1 tsp baking soda

1 Preheat the oven to 200°C/400°F. Line a deep 12-hole muffin tray with paper baking cups. Wash and dry the cherries. Chop them roughly, mix them with the chocolate chips and set aside.

2 Beat the margarine and sugar together, then whisk in the eggs, yogurt, and milk. Sift in the flour and baking soda. Stir until just combined.

3 Fold in three quarters of the cherries and chocolate chips. Spoon the mixture into the baking cups, filling them two-thirds full. Sprinkle the remaining cherries and chocolate chips over the top.

4 Bake for about 20 minutes until golden and firm. Leave in the pans for 4 minutes, then turn out to cool on a wire rack.

Chocolate Oat Bars

Makes 24

215 g/7½ oz/1¾ cups
   all-purpose flour
150 g/5 oz/1¼ cups rolled oats
225 g/8 oz/1 cup
   light brown sugar
1 tsp baking soda

pinch salt
150 g/5 oz/⅔ cup butter
2 tbsp corn syrup
250 g/9 oz/9 squares dark
   unsweetened chocolate
5 tbsp heavy cream

1 Preheat the oven to 180°C/350°F, 10 minutes before baking. Lightly oil a 33 x 23-cm/ 13 x 9-inch jelly roll pan and line with nonstick parchment paper. Place the flour, rolled oats, light brown sugar, baking soda, and salt into a bowl and stir well together.

2 Melt the butter and corn syrup together in a heavy saucepan and stir until smooth, then add to the oat mixture and mix together thoroughly. Spoon the mixture into the prepared pan, press down firmly, and level the top.

3 Bake in the preheated oven for 15–20 minutes or until golden. Remove from the oven and let cool in the pan. Once cool, remove from the pan. Discard the parchment.

4 Melt the chocolate in a heatproof bowl set over a saucepan of gently simmering water (make sure the bowl doesn't touch the water). Alternatively, melt the chocolate in the microwave according to the manufacturer's instructions. Once the chocolate has melted, quickly beat in the cream, then pour over the oat bars. Mark patterns over the chocolate with a fork when almost set.

5 Chill the oat bars in the refrigerator for at least 30 minutes before cutting into sections. When the chocolate has set, serve. Store in an airtight container for a few days.

Gingerbread Cookies

Makes 20 large or 28 small cookies

225 g/8 oz/1¾ cups all-purpose flour, plus extra for dusting

½ tsp ground ginger

½ tsp mixed spice

½ tsp baking soda

75 g/3 oz/⅓ cup (6 tbsp) butter

2 tbsp corn syrup

1 tbsp molasses

75 g/3 oz/⅓ cup soft dark brown sugar

50 g/2 oz/scant ½ cup royal-icing sugar, to decorate

1 Preheat the oven to 180°C/350°F and grease two baking sheets. Sift the flour, spices, and baking soda into a bowl.

2 Place the butter, syrup, molasses, and sugar in a heavy-based pan with 1 tablespoon water and heat gently until every grain of sugar has dissolved and the butter has melted. Cool for 5 minutes, then pour the melted mixture into the dry ingredients and mix to a soft dough.

3 Leave the dough, covered, for 30 minutes. Roll out the dough on a lightly floured surface to a 3 mm/⅛ inch thickness and cut out fancy shapes. Gather up the trimmings and re-roll the dough, cutting out more shapes. Place on the baking sheets using a spatula and bake for about 10 minutes until golden and firm. Be careful not to overcook, as the cookies will brown quickly.

4 Decorate the cookies by mixing the royal-icing sugar with enough water to make a piping consistency. Place the icing in a small paper piping bag with the end snipped away and pipe faces and decorations on to the cookies.

Pumpkin Cookies with Brown Butter Glaze

Makes 48

125 g/4 oz/½ cup
butter, softened

150 g/5 oz/1¼ cups
all-purpose flour

175 g/6 oz/¾ cup lightly packed,
light brown sugar

225 g/8 oz/1 cup canned
pumpkin or cooked pumpkin

1 egg, beaten

2 tsp ground cinnamon

2½ tsp vanilla extract

½ tsp baking powder

½ tsp baking soda

½ tsp freshly grated nutmeg

125 g/4 oz/1 scant cup
whole-wheat flour

100 g/3½ oz/½ cup raisins

75 g/3 oz/¾ cup pecans,
roughly chopped

50 g/2 oz/¼ cup unsalted butter

225 g/8 oz/2 cups
confectioners' sugar

2 tbsp milk

1 Preheat the oven to 190°C/375°F, 10 minutes before baking. Lightly oil a baking sheet and reserve.

2 Using an electric mixer, beat the butter until light and fluffy. Add the flour, sugar, pumpkin, and beaten egg and beat with the mixer until mixed well. Stir in the ground cinnamon, 1 teaspoon of the vanilla extract and then sift in the baking powder, baking soda, and grated nutmeg. Beat the mixture until combined well, scraping down the sides of the bowl. Add the whole-wheat flour, chopped nuts, and raisins to the mixture and fold in with a metal spoon or rubber spatula until mixed thoroughly together.

3 Place teaspoonfuls about 5 cm/2 inches apart onto the baking sheet. Bake in the preheated oven for 10–12 minutes, or until the cookie edges are firm.

4 Remove the cookies from the oven and let cool on a wire rack. Meanwhile, melt the butter in a small saucepan over a medium heat, until pale and just turning golden brown.

5 Remove from the heat. Add the sugar, remaining vanilla extract, and milk, stirring. Drizzle over the cooled cookies and serve.

Chocolate & Nut Refrigerator Cookies

Makes 18

165 g/5½ oz/1½ sticks slightly
    salted butter
150 g/5 oz/⅔ cup soft dark
    brown sugar
25 g/1 oz/2 tbsp
    granulated sugar

1 medium egg, beaten
200 g/7 oz/1¾ cups
    all-purpose flour
½ tsp baking soda
25 g/1 oz/¼ cup cocoa powder
125 g/4 oz/1 cup pecan nuts,
    finely chopped

1 Cream 150 g/5 oz of the butter and both sugars in a large bowl until light and fluffy, then gradually beat in the egg.

2 Sift the flour, baking soda, and cocoa powder together, then gradually fold into the creamed mixture together with the chopped pecans. Mix thoroughly until a smooth but stiff dough is formed.

3 Place the dough on a lightly floured surface or pastry board and roll into sausage shapes about 5 cm/2 inches in diameter. Wrap in plastic wrap and chill in the refrigerator for at least 12 hours, or preferably overnight.

4 Preheat the oven to 190°C/375°F, 10 minutes before baking. Lightly grease several baking sheets with the remaining butter. Cut the dough into thin slices and place on the prepared baking sheets. Bake in the preheated oven for 8–10 minutes until firm. Remove from the oven and leave to cool slightly. Using a spatula, transfer to a wire rack to cool. Store in an airtight container.

Oatmeal Raisin Cookies

Makes 24

175 g/6 oz/1½ cups all-purpose flour

150 g/5 oz/2 cups rolled oats

1 tsp ground ginger

½ tsp baking powder

½ tsp baking soda

125 g/4 oz/⅔ cup demerara/turbinado sugar

50 g/2 oz/⅓ cup raisins

1 large egg, lightly beaten

150 ml/¼ pint/⅔ cup vegetable or sunflower/corn oil

4 tbsp milk

1 Preheat the oven to 200°C/400°F, 15 minutes before baking. Lightly grease a baking sheet.

2 Mix together the flour, oats, ground ginger, baking powder, baking soda, sugar, and the raisins in a large bowl.

3 In another bowl, mix the egg, oil, and milk together. Make a well in the center of the dry ingredients and pour in the egg mixture.

4 Mix the mixture together well with either a fork or a wooden spoon to make a soft but not sticky dough.

5 Place spoonfuls of the dough well apart on the greased baking sheet and flatten the tops down slightly with the tines of a fork.

6 Transfer the cookies to the preheated oven and bake for 10–12 minutes until golden.

7 Remove from the oven, leave to cool for 2–3 minutes, then transfer the cookies to a wire rack to cool. Serve when cold or otherwise store in an airtight container.

Further Reading

Briggs, M., *Bicarbonate of Soda: A Very Versatile Natural Substance*, Black and White Publishing, 2007

Briggs, M., *Green Cleaning: Natural Hints and Tips*, Abbeydale Press, 2008

Briggs, M., *Vinegar – 1001 Practical Uses*, Abbeydale Press, 2006

Constantino, M., *Household Hints*, Flame Tree, 2009

Fraser, R., *Neal's Yard Remedies Recipes for Natural Beauty*, Haldane Mason Ltd, 2007

Grace, J. L., *Imperfectly Natural Home: The Organic Bible*, Orion, 2008

Hamilton, A., *The Self Sufficient-ish Bible*, Hodder & Stoughton, 2009

Harrison, J., *Low-Cost Living: Live better, spend less*, Right Way, 2009

Lansky, V., *Baking Soda: Over 500 Fabulous, Fun, and Frugal Uses You've Probably Never Thought of*, Book Peddlers, 2008

Logan, K.N., *Clean House, Clean Planet: Clean Your House for Pennies a Day, the Safe, Nontoxic Way*, Simon & Schuster, 1997

Martin, A., *Natural Stain Remover: Clean Your Home Without Harmful Chemicals*, Apple Press, 2003

Peacock, D., *Good Home Cooking: Make it, Don't Buy It! Real Food at Home – Mostly at Less Than a Pound a Head*, Spring Hill 2009

Peacock, P., *Grandma's Ways for Modern Days: Relearning Traditional Self-sufficiency – Gardening, Cooking and Household Management*, Spring Hill, 2009

Reader's Digest, *Extraordinary Uses For Ordinary Things: 2,209 Ways to Save Money and Time*, Reader's Digest, 2008

Reader's Digest, *1001 Home Remedies: Trustworthy Treatments for Everyday Health Problems*, Reader's Digest, 2005

Strawbridge, D., & Strawbridge, J., *Practical Self Sufficiency: The Complete Guide to Sustainable Living*, Dorling Kindersley, 2010

Websites

www.armhammer.com
The official website for the Arm & Hammer baking soda company. It offers practical uses for baking soda, including a section on projects for kids.

www.babycentre.co.uk
A website that offers plenty of advice about caring for babies from pregnancy to preschool.

www.channel4.com/food/recipes/baking
A website that offers many baking ideas, including many recipes that involve baking soda.

www.doityourself.com
A website that offers various DIY tips and projects.

www.enjo.org.uk
A website that offers chemical-free, environmentally friendly cleaning products for all areas of the home.

www.healthy-holistic-living.com
A website devoted to holistic living as a path to improvements in physical, spiritual and mental wellbeing. There is even a section on baking soda!

www.hygieneexpert.co.uk
A website that offers hygiene advice and information for humans as well as pets.

www.gardenersworld.com
A website with tips and guides for gardeners of any experience level.

www.grist.org
An environmentally conscious news site that gives tips on DIY projects and green living.

www.home-remedies-for-you.com
A website that offers treatments for a plethora of ailments using common household products, including good old baking soda.

www.treehugger.com
A website that focuses entirely on green living. It contains news about the latest environmentally friendly technology as well as advice on how to make a positive environmental impact.

www.ultimatehandyman.co.uk
A website that offers advice on do-it-yourself home improvement and gives instructions on undertaking many household DIY projects.

www.wackyuses.com
A website that offers unusual but helpful uses for common household products.

Picture Credits

The following images are © **Foundry Arts**: 259, 263 (both Paul Forrester), 288, and 291–313. All other images are courtesy of **Shutterstock** and © the following photographers: 1 & 249, 4t & 46 & 53, 218, 275 Monkey Business Images; 3 & 169, 170 auremar; 48, 144–45 digieye; 4b & 191 Karen H. Ilgan; 4c & 117 Anthony Harris; 55, 81 Baloncici; 5c & 247 HP_photo; 5t & 219 Gemenacom; 6 & 146 & 157, 50, 134, 179 Diego Cervo; 7 Andre Klaassen; 8, 127 Picsfive; 9, 12–13 matka_Wariatka; 10 Jonathan Vasata; 11 & 167 Kurhan; 14 & 23, 175 Julija Sapic; 15 oleksa ; 16 Victoria Alexandrova; 17, 18 Photoroller; 19, 257 Irina Fischer; 20 margouillat photo; 21 Tom Baker; 22 Chris Harvey; 24 artproem; 25 M.E. Mulder; 26 Daniel Krylov; 27 James M Phelps Jr; 29 Ragne Kabanova; 30 UlianaSt; 31 jokerpro; 32 Michael Perrigrew; 33 Anne Kitzman; 35 Tomasz Trojanowski; 36 HABRDA; 37 Olivier Le Queinec; 38 Pavelk; 39 Paul Cowan; 40 sjeacle; 41 Muriel Lasure; 42 Lepas; 43 Cheryl Casey; 44 SasPartout; 45 Vadym Drobot; 47 yampi; 48 Brian A Jackson; 51 Crystal Kirk; 52 Tiplyashin Anatoly; 54 Alistair Scott; 56 Freerk Brouwer; 57 Yellowj; 58 Paul Maguire; 59 Daniel Goodings; 60 & 63, 64 Konovalikov Andrey; 61 Gorin; 62 aceshot1; 65 terekhov igor; 66 Margo Harrison; 67 michaeljung; 68 Kimberly Hall; 69, 119 Peter Gudella; 70, 149 jkitan; 71 Joe Belanger; 72 Lori Sparkia; 73, 213 Jaimie Duplass; 75 Terry Underwood Evans; 76 Freddy Eliasson; 77 Shane White; 78 Yuri Arcurs; 79 Olga Chernetskaya; 80 khz; 82 Darren A Hubley; 83 Maria Dryfhout; 85 Leifstiller; 86 Alkristeena; 87 PAUL ATKINSON; 88 Matt Ragen; 89, 193 Zholobov Vadim; 90 & 349 Germany Feng; 91 Supri Suharjoto; 92 Paul Matthew Photography; 93 Lisa Turay; 95 ushama; 96 Romanchuk Dimitry; 97 Maridav; 99 Nagy Jozsef - Attila; 100tl Marie C. Fields; 100br trailexlorers; 101 photogl; 102 & 109 Carrieanne Larmore; 103 Vuk Nenezic; 104 Baevskiy Dmitry; 105 & 315 Michelle D Milliman; 106 iofoto; 107 Slasha; 108 Onur ERSIN; 110tl Joy Brown; 110br Tootles; 111 Sarah Salmela; 112 Thomas Skjæveland; 113 MattJones; 114–15 ZTS; 116 & 123 pixelman; 118 Toranico; 120 Shantell photographe; 121, 228 teekaygee; 122 Joseph; 124 Igor Dutina; 125 Eric Gevaert; 126 Paul Krugloff; 128 Karkas; 129 Petro Feketa; 130 Danylchenko

Iaroslav; 131 Agb; 132 Martin Smith; 133 Babusi Octavian Florentin; 135 Jean Valley; 136 Dan Thomas Brostrom; 137 Mirco Vacca; 138 James Coleman; 139 easyshoot; 140 & 142 Stephen VanHorn; 141 Andersr; 143 Dmitriy Yakovlev; 147 rebvt; 148, 289 Piotr Marcinski; 150 Rene Jansa; 151 Arie v.d. Wolde; 152 pzAxe; 153 Skazka Grez; 154 Danijel Micka; 155 Liv friis-larsen; 156 Poznyakov; 158 Tania Zbrodko; 159 Nicolas Dufresne; 160 Subbotina Anna ; 161 Anthony Berenyi; 162 Alexey Stiop; 163 Netfalls; 164 imageshunter; 165 kristian sekulic; 166 Camilo Torres; 168 Alexa Catalin; 171 StockLite; 172 paul prescott; 173 Levent Konuk; 174 sevenke; 176 Natthawat Wongrat ; 177, 194 & 199 Elena Elisseeva; 178 GraÃ§a Victoria ; 180 & 189 Vasina Natalia; 181 elaine hudson; 182 charles taylor; 183 Wojciech Zbieg; 184 Gaby Kooijman; 185 Artur Bogacki; 186 Kristy Pargeter; 187 Zsolt Nyulaszi; 188r James R T Bossert; 188l Kafer photo; 192, 244 & 261 Ieva Geneciviene; 195 Edw; 196 gsplanet; 197 Miodrag Gajic; 198 Melinda Fawver; 200 Jirsak; 201, 267 Noam Armonn; 202 Joe Gough; 203 Tobik; 204–205 efirm; 206 & 209 Vasily Mulyukin; 207 Scott L. Williams; 210 david n madden; 211 kreego; 212 Nancy Kennedy; 214 Cristi Lucaci; 215 Kimmit; 216 Cherick; 217 Stuart Monk; 220 dendong; 221 Alena Ozerova; 222 Alena Brozova; 223 Pakhnyushcha; 224 Ivonne Wierink; 225 Vakhrushev Pavel; 226 Johanna Goodyear; 227 Andrey Pavlov; 228 Vaclav Volrab; 230 Ramona Heim; 231 Mona Makela; 232 Christina Richards; 233 Losevsky Pavel; 234 & 241 Dmitry Naumov; 235 SNEHIT; 236 Kathy Piper; 237 Jason Stitt; 238 Pedro Salaverria; 239 yazan masa; 240 Matej Pavlansky; 242–43 Kruchankova Maya; 245 Aleksandar-Pal Sakala; 246 Alex Staroseltsev; 248, 254, 284 Thomas M Perkins; 250 Yurchyks; 251 Serghei Starus; 253 Robert Anthony; 255 Renata Osinska; 258 Morgar; 260 travis manley; 262 bierchen; 264 Roxana Bashyrova; 265 Whitechild; 266 holbox; 268–69, 278tr Magdalena Kucova; 270 & 283 Tyler Olson; 271 Ermes; 272 Jacek Chabraszewski; 273 David P. Smith; 276 Richard Griffin; 277 Rey Kamensky; 278bl Mark Plumley; 279 jathys; 280 Aleksandra Duda; 281 Denis and Yulia Pogostins; 285 Elke Dennis; 286 Valeriy Velikov; 287 Viktor1.

Index